Leading the
High-Performing Company

Leading the High-Performing Company

A Transformational Guide to Growing Your Business and Outperforming Your Competition

Heidi Pozzo

 BUSINESS EXPERT PRESS

First published in 2018 by
Business Expert Press, LLC
222 East 46th Street, New York, NY 10017
www.businessexpertpress.com

ISBN-13: 978-1-94784-335-6 (paperback)
ISBN-13: 978-1-94784-336-3 (e-book)

Business Expert Press Human Resource Management and Organizational Behavior Collection

Collection ISSN: 1946-5637 (print)
Collection ISSN: 1946-5645 (electronic)

Cover and interior design by S4Carlisle Publishing Services Private Ltd., Chennai, India

First edition: 2018

10 9 8 7 6 5 4 3 2 1

Printed in the United States of America.

Advanced Quotes for
Leading the High-Performing Company

Leading the High-Performing Company is an essential guide for leaders who want their company to achieve new heights and grow as a leader. *Leading* captures the symbiotic nature of leaders and the businesses they lead, providing practical tools for both to be at their best.

> Marshall Goldsmith
> *Thinkers 50* World's #1 Executive Coach
> #6 Most Influential Business Thinker 2017

I found *Leading the High Performing Company* to be an insightful and useful guide for both current and aspiring leaders. It provides essential and practical advice for effectively establishing and communicating a vision, engaging all stakeholders and measuring success. Whether launching a new venture or leading a Fortune 500 company, *Leading the High Performing Company* provides the reader with essential tools that will show them how to take the organization to the next level.

> Tom Christie
> *retired partner EY*

Leading the High-Performing Company will challenge you to focus on the execution of and accountability to your business strategy, and constant innovative thought in good times and bad. Heidi Pozzo's performance accelerators, including examples from her experiences and philosophies as well as other acclaimed leaders, will help you reflect on the impact your leadership style has on more than success in business alone. Her insights will reveal the impact you have on the many lives influenced by your daily actions, from employees to clients to your community, and is a must read to find your purpose and shape the legacy you hope to leave in the wake of your leadership.

> Steve Fein
> *Regional Managing Partner, Oregon, Moss Adams*

Heidi's passion for leadership is evident from page one. Her book is a comprehensive guide, taking you through a logical progression of fundamentals that are spot on, from leadership and team development to defining your competitive edge. For those in a new leadership position, this will be a valuable tool. For seasoned leaders, you will be reminded to address those key areas that are sometimes ignored but so important to future success. Thanks for those reminders Heidi!

Erick Frack
CEO, Enoch Precision Machining

I liked what I read! Heidi crafted a simple, easy to understand guide to leading a high-performing business. And it is not just for leaders—if you are an operator it all makes sense. In business, the name of the game is People and Communication. Heidi provides practical tips for how to communicate and bring the best out in your people. And she outlines how to focus on what matters. I love FOCUS—it is what drives results.

Tony Arnerich
CEO, Arnerich Massena

Whether you are a front-line employee or a C-Level Executive, Leading the High Performance Company should be on your list of must reads! This book simplifies the sometimes overly academic approach to building a high-performance organization. The author strategically places insights from effective leaders and calls-to-action throughout the book to force the reader to be both honest and introspective when analyzing themselves and their organization. Well done Heidi!

Corey McCort
Chief Operating Officer, Carson

I am truly impressed with *Leading the High-Performing Company*. It is the book every MBA program should require. Leadership is multi-faceted and this book helps to identify the dimensions of top leaders while providing examples that reinforce the concepts and a roadmap to lead the reader towards developing their own leadership talents. Recognizing that leadership is about the relationships you develop with people inside and outside your organization is a concept that is lost on many. Many can imitate your product or service. But by creating a unique set of high quality relationships with employees, customers, vendors and the community surrounding the company, the leader creates a set of resources than cannot be imitated. This book elevates this fundamental precept. Leaders who follow the guidance here will find not only a stronger organization but many ancillary benefits they could not have anticipated.

Jane Cote
Academic Director, Carson College of Business,
Washington State University Vancouver

Leadership has a profound impact on the performance of a business. Heidi highlights the critical decision points leaders encounter while building and leading teams. Filled with insights and practical tools, *Leading* provides a roadmap for leaders to become high-performing. Whether new to leading or a seasoned leader, everyone will find something to put into practice today.

Geoff Telfer
Senior Vice President,
Corporate Finance and Investor Relations, Fluor

Successful leadership is a broad term with confusing multitude of requirements. Heidi Pozzo has been able to artfully organize a core set of concepts under the heading of *Leading The High-Performing Company*. The unique value of this book is the clarity it provides for new leaders while simultaneously offering new insights for seasoned CEOs. The book is very well structured uncluttering important leadership considerations into 11 chapters. In each area, Heidi provides illustrative examples, clear guidelines, and an actionable list under "Pozzo Accelerators" heading. Throughout the book, Heidi manages to balance the short-term business performance with long-term people investments while avoiding the tired cliches so common in business publications. This book is an easy read and belongs in the reference library for all who aspire to lead their organizations to outperform their competition.

Ron Khormaei, PhD
VP of Engineering, SawStop LLC;
Adjunct Professor, Portland State University;
CoFounder/CEO, FINEX Cast Iron Cookware Co.

High performing companies do not get there by mistake. The key, as highlighted in *Leading the High-Performing Company*, is knowledgeable, dedicated and enthusiastic leadership that know how to leverage their assets—people, equipment, intellectual property or capital. Whether it is a startup, a turnaround or a growth plan for an already great company, they all require a well thought out strategy, a clear and concise implementation plan and the right form of communication and buy in at all levels of the organization from the Board to all levels of staff. Clear goals are set, performance measures put in place and routine progress reports conducted along the way. Heidi provides a roadmap outlining each of these steps in *Leading*.

As Heidi highlights, most successful leaders share many positive traits. The really good ones are those that realize that there are always new things to learn and are always trying to grow personally. They almost always surround themselves with bright people with varying skill sets that can deliver the desired change and culture. High performance is not just about the profits. If the culture is right, the talent is developed and the strategy is managed well, the profits will follow. Working in those environments can be magic.

Ron Oakley
Retired Engineering and Construction CEO

Abstract

Why do some companies thrive—even through vast changes or market volatility?

What differentiates *high-performing* companies from those that *just get by*?

Leading The High-Performing Company demystifies performance. This transformational guide provides the crucial tools and insights to grow your business and outperform peers. It pinpoints how successful leaders and companies position themselves to lead in their industries.

Explore the symbiotic nature of leaders and the businesses they lead. Learn why life is better for everyone when the business is performing at its best. Discover the actions necessary to leverage your organization to new heights and grow as a leader.

This book is based on the author's professional career—leading at an executive level and working with high-performing organizations through the good and bad times. Real-world examples bring the concepts to life based on the experiences of the author, as well as accomplished leaders, including Jim Hackett, Stephen Babson, Alan Weiss, Mitzi Perdue, Wendy Collie, Brian Ferriso, and Tom Hellie. You'll walk away with actionable insights to accelerate your business today.

Keywords

focus, high-performing, leadership, outperform, personal best, purpose, success, team, top talent, transformation

Contents

Acknowledgments

Many people have helped me develop the insights shared in this book over many years. I am thankful to them for years of lessons and insights. Many others have shared their experience of taking a book from a thought to completion. Alan Weiss and his community were instrumental in developing my book proposal and taking it through completion. Thanks to Jocelyn Godfrey Carbonara, Val Wright, Paul Rulkens, Jim Grew, and Sally Strackbein for playing key roles in shaping this book. Special thanks to the leaders who shared their time and insights with me. Thank you!

Insights from Accomplished Leaders

In writing this book, several accomplished leaders shared their insights into the distinctive qualities of high-performing leaders and organizations. They all worked very hard to gain mastery, are passionate about what they do, and have tapped into an energy source that fuels them. I am grateful to them for sharing their wisdom and insight with me. You'll see their stories throughout this book. Following is more about their unique backgrounds.

Stephen Babson

Stephen Babson is managing director of Endeavour Capital, a private-equity firm based in the Pacific Northwest. With degrees in English, business, and the law, Stephen has a unique perspective. His liberal arts background has clearly given him a leg up in recognizing patterns in business that stretch across many industries. It is the ability to see those patterns with an industry overlay that allows him to be successful in many industries.

Stephen grew up in a family steeped in music and the arts. This was foundational to his right-brained instincts. He realized he had to become more left-brained to be successful in his career and education. And that forced him to learn the fundamentals of business in a deeper and more deliberate way.

His own values, as well as those of Endeavour, focus on the long term and leaving companies better off than before he was involved. It is clear that the people he chooses to work with have mutually selected him with the goal to grow long-term businesses that create value for everyone involved. And this approach has led to a successful career.

Wendy Collie

Wendy Collie is a purposeful leader whose perspectives about successful businesses originate with her father. An entrepreneurial man, her father built a thriving HVAC business in Southern California in the 1950s, before air-conditioning was widely available. He knew that business was about more than just profitability. It was about people. Treating his employees with respect and trust, he shared the success of the company in the good times with his people, and his people would work together during the tough times to stay afloat.

Wendy took this perspective into her leadership roles at Starbucks and as CEO of New Seasons Market, a neighborhood grocery chain in the Pacific Northwest. Her time at Starbucks was particularly impactful as she was mentored by Howard Behar in servant leadership, the belief that leaders who place the needs of their people first create high-performing teams and results. She gravitated toward businesses that believed in more than just selling a product or service—but rather an experience: A touch point between the customer, product, community, and people in the company.

Understanding that people want more than just a job, they want a sense of purpose, she puts purpose at the center of the organizations she leads. While her list of accomplishments is long, she is most proud of creating the circumstances for people to realize their full potential and be fulfilled. By putting people first, including them in their own development, and encouraging them to trust in themselves, she has seen remarkable things happen in the most extraordinary ways.

Brian Ferriso

Brian Ferriso has been at the helm of the Portland Art Museum since 2006. During his tenure, he has focused the organization on offering three pillars—art of quality and importance, access for all, and strong fiscal accountability. As a result, membership and attendance have grown, and the curatorial staff of premier scholars in their area has doubled. The Rothko Pavilion, a $50 million expansion connecting the two buildings and enhancing the experience, is currently underway.

With all he has accomplished, you may be surprised to hear his undergraduate degree was in economics. After interviewing with the investment bank Salomon Brothers, he decided that it was not the career path for him. He loved being around the creative process and began teaching high school art. He found his passion there and returned to school for a master's degree in arts administration and a master's degree in art history. His interest in how the business world and principles could be used in the museum world to further its evolution ignited him and launched his career.

Jim Hackett

Jim Hackett has been so successful in business that he was funded in 2017 with a $3.8 billion blank check to acquire an oil explorer and pipeline firm. His success as chairman and CEO of Anadarko created the foundation for his current venture. His list of accomplishments and board positions is long, and his insights show it. As CEO at this oil and gas company, he lifts the people in the company up and rewards the people and the shareholders for their respective contributions.

Jim believes it is important to do good and engage with society. His views on faith, accountability, and discipline were formed through his early life and while at a military academy. Those views were reinforced when Enron collapsed, devastating many people in its wake. To further explore what had been a life of studying divinity informally, he went to Harvard Divinity School to further his studies. He is a strong believer in faith-based leadership—believing that being accountable to a higher power provides a moral anchor to do good. And that is how he lives his life.

Note: In reading this book, you will also see reference to Jim Hackett at Ford. These are two different men.

Tom Hellie

Tom Hellie spent his career in higher education, most recently as the president of Linfield College. During his time there, he doubled the size of the endowment, doubled the size of its nursing school, tripled the enrollment of people of color, and launched a liberal-arts-based wine studies program.

What might surprise you is his early career as a theater professor and director of plays. He very cleverly draws parallels between directing a play—articulating a vision and getting people to work together as a team—and being a college administrator. His passion has always centered around having an impact on people's lives and making the world better. He found he could do that through education.

Between his time at the Associated Colleges of the Midwest, the Kemper Foundation, and Linfield College, he gained a keen insight into the culture of organizations and how well their leaders fit. For Tom, cultural fit is a defining factor—so much so that he has made cultural fit a central focus in building teams.

Mitzi Perdue

The daughter of the founder of Sheraton Hotels and wife of Frank Perdue, founder of Perdue Chicken, Mitzi has firsthand insight into scaling successful businesses. But her experience doesn't stop there. She has built several successful businesses of her own. She founded and grew several agricultural businesses and is a speaker and author.

Her career and life have included developing networks of people that together create new solutions. She is a lifelong learner, describing herself as an informavore. She feeds on information, attends conferences, and puts herself in the way of interesting people. Like Stephen Babson, she has been able to recognize patterns and apply them to business to create leading-edge approaches. She does this by spotting good ideas and taking the concepts into her business and life.

Alan Weiss

Alan Weiss is an entrepreneur who has carved out a corner of the consulting world. He is so dominant in the industry that he has more than 60 books on the topic and has created a community that stretches around the world. He has mentored thousands of people in how to create successful practices.

With a career that spans beyond 40 years, Alan has unique insights into what makes individual leaders tick and how that impacts their businesses. He has constantly reinvented himself over the course of his career. In doing so, he has managed to intertwine his work and personal lives together, giving him the ability to make a significant impact with his customers while having an abundance of time to focus on what he values.

Introduction

After more than two decades of working with high-performing companies (and those that are not), I've seen firsthand the impact business has on the lives of its people and communities, both good and bad. And I've experienced the factors that differentiate high-performing companies—and their leaders.

Successful transformations toward becoming a high-performing company, in particular, can have a tremendous positive impact. By moving from underperforming or performing on par with competitors, an organization is required to fundamentally improve every aspect of the business. That means everyone who touches the business has a better experience.

Having led this type of transformation, I know what it takes to get there.

I've also seen the devastating impact of a series of mistakes—resulting in major layoffs and bankruptcy. The mistakes start with not keeping pace with the industry and losing competitiveness. Leaders miss turns in the economy and don't react quickly enough. And as a result, people lose their jobs without notice and have no bridge to support their livelihood.

Leadership and focus matter to a company's performance—especially when that company is going through change or needs to transform its approach. Throughout my career, I've been fortunate to work with extraordinary leaders. These leaders shared some key traits. Each of them knew the drivers of the business and what levers needed to be pulled to achieve success. They understood the interrelationship of all the moving parts that needed to work in concert to achieve and outperform expectations.

The decisions they grappled with the most were those that directly impacted the lives and employment of the people in the organization. The weight of these decisions rested clearly on their shoulders. People weren't just numbers on a sheet of paper; they were friends with families that depended upon employment. Any changes to staffing levels were considered with great thought, and at times agony.

Later in my career, those experiences weighed on my mind, as I was responsible for making changes that impacted the business and the lives of the people—both within the organization and in the community.

It was through experiencing the ups and downs of business that I came to deeply appreciate how a well-run company can lift up all that it touches. Businesses exist in an ecosystem that comprises the business, the community, the people who work in the business, and the stakeholders of the business. The strength of the business has a profound impact on those that it touches. As the business becomes more successful, it employs more people and generates a host of benefits in the community and for stakeholders.

Customers are delighted with the products or services, people who work for the company are engaged and go home satisfied on most days, the investors see a strong return, and the community benefits from a healthy economy.

Businesses that are not run well can have a devastating effect on the lives of the people and the communities in which they exist. Even if they don't go bankrupt, the level of stress experienced follows the people home.

Leading the High-Performing Company highlights what leaders and companies that outperform do to set themselves apart from those that perform well below expectations. It explores the symbiotic nature of leaders and the businesses they lead. It demonstrates why life is better for everyone when the business is performing at its best. And it highlights the actions needed to get there.

Leaders of companies that outperform investor expectations understand how those companies fit in the ecosystem. They understand what attracts people to their business. They look internally and externally and constantly challenge themselves to get better. And that starts with leaders sharing a personal philosophy. *Leading the High-Performing Company* provides the roadmap to get there.

Each chapter has success stories along with insights into the actions that drove the success of the business or leader. While each chapter stands alone, the combined elements from all the chapters are necessary to outperform expectations. Tools are included in each for the readers to utilize on their journey.

At times, *Leading the High-Performing Company* will challenge you to step back and think deeply. It may challenge your beliefs. Growing and innovating take constant learning and challenging of your beliefs and the values of your business. Challenging your thinking and beliefs should be uncomfortable at times. This book should push you out of your comfort zone and challenge you to a new level of thinking and performance management.

I'm passionate about this topic because I believe that a rising tide lifts all boats. If we can collectively strengthen ourselves and our businesses, everyone will benefit. I hope you are passionate about this too.

Whether you are a leader today, or want to become one in the future, you will find practical tips and tools for taking your organization to the next level. As senior leaders, you have the ability to make broad organizational changes. If your leadership role is somewhere in the middle, you can bring many of these concepts into your organization. If you are not yet in a formal leadership role but strive to make an impact as a leader in the future, these concepts will give you a foundation for what drives the best companies.

In high-performing organizations, good ideas come from everywhere. With a compelling case, you may be able to lead the introduction of these concepts more broadly. You may also find that people take note of what you are doing and adopt your actions more broadly.

Before we jump into the rest of the book, take a moment to shift your perspective to *what can be* and *how you will make it happen.*

CHAPTER 1

High-Performing Leadership

Why do some businesses perform better than others?

I believe it all comes down to *leadership and focus*. Throughout my career, I've been fortunate to work with incredible leaders and be a part of amazing transformation stories—transforming companies that were not living up to their potential into high-performing organizations.

I've also seen some challenging circumstances.

Leaders can take any circumstance and lift an organization up, engage the people, and deliver results. They know the difference between being lucky due to market conditions and running the business well. They don't take credit for growth driven by a strong economy. Rather, they drive growth in a down economy.

My career has taken me from small businesses to Fortune 500 businesses—privately held, publicly held, and private-equity owned. Regardless of the size or ownership structure of the organization, there is a consistency in leadership that outperforms. And without that leadership, a vacuum develops that causes the company to revert to less optimal performance.

Leadership is everything.

Leadership is the difference between a company going bankrupt and being wildly successful. The direction set by leadership determines the outcome.

To be a high-performing business, high-performing leaders must be present to set the direction and focus of the organization. It is not possible to have a high-performing business without high-performing leadership. We'll delve into what those leaders do that is distinctive and results in high-performing businesses.

I'll share insights about what works and what doesn't based on my own experience, and insights from leaders I admire and businesses that have made the journey.

What Does a High-Performing Business Look Like?

You can recognize high-performing businesses initially by their outward appearance. Regardless of the industry, the facilities are clean and well lit. The office space is comfortable and conducive to work. Manufacturing facilities are well laid out, safe, and facilitate the flow of work. Facilities, equipment, and technology are reasonably up to date and facilitate the business operations.

The people are engaged and enjoy coming to work. People work collaboratively across the organization. You can walk through the business and ask any person about its purpose and goals, and you will receive an answer that is consistent across the organization.

Goals are widely discussed, people understand how they came about, and they are reported against regularly. And not just by management. People up and down the organization own their part and are accountable for results.

Customers and suppliers are engaged at a level beyond just an order. Relationships are in place at many levels across the organization and in a manner that allows for collaboration and adjustments up and down in business size. There are no surprises.

A culture of innovation and learning exists such that resources are dedicated toward business growth. They are not disconnected from the organization, but an integral part that feeds off continuous feedback from sales, operations, customers, suppliers, and market conditions. Work gets done fast. Decision making happens quickly with all relevant information considered; people move quickly to act. Systems and processes are streamlined and support the business. You'll never hear people complaining that it is taking too long to get a decision made or that they are waiting for the system to get work done.

There is a clear focus driven by leadership around the purpose of the business and its goals. The values become part of the culture. People are responsible and accountable—they own their piece of the business. And it all starts with leadership.

Does your business look like this? Can you think of another business that does? A division of a business?

Early in my career, I was fortunate to be part of a high-performing business. I worked as a teller in a credit union in downtown Los Angeles.

The team was diverse, yet cohesive, and enjoyed working together. As you can imagine in any retail location, there would be an influx of customers, and a line would form. Quickly, everyone would pitch in to make sure people were helped in a friendly and expeditious manner. Customer satisfaction was always high.

Many years later, I was a key leader in the transformation of Longview Fibre Paper and Packaging, Inc., a pulp and paper, and corrugated box business located in the Pacific Northwest. The transformation was so successful, it was considered a "textbook example" of restructuring an old-line business. According to Deutsche Bank analyst Mark Wilde, it was "the best turnaround case study we have seen in the past 25 years."

But Longview wasn't always that way. It took years of working on all the components outlined in this book to become a high-performing business.

The High-Performing Business

High-performing—what does that mean, and how do you achieve it? Even if you don't hold a formal leadership position today, learning the concepts that go into such an organization will help you thrive in your area and ultimately achieve a leadership position, if desired.

Performance can be measured in a variety of ways: It could be based on the longevity of the company, financial performance, or stock price. Today, other measures, such as social responsibility and diversity, are included as well.

Investors are increasingly looking at the holistic performance of companies in evaluating performance and allocating capital. They are looking for companies having strong financial performance, as well as a positive impact on their ecosystem.

The reality is, companies that outperform know that in order to produce strong financial results, they must be the top choice for customers, have top talent that works together, and do the right things in business every day. Leadership is the means to achieving top performance.

So what does that mean in terms of evaluating performance? Should one use market valuation? Or revenue (which is what *Fortune* uses to determine its company rankings)? What about longevity? Or earnings per share (EPS)? How does the valuation of different sectors come into play when thinking about how to evaluate performance? And what about nonfinancial measures? The long and short of it is, there are many ways to evaluate performance.

It is helpful to get to the basics when evaluating performance. Every business needs cash to operate. Revenue without cash generation is OK in a start-up, as long as there is a path to success. But long term, a business is not successful by merely selling products or services. Its revenue must exceed the cost of running the business to generate cash and be sustainable. For a business to operate in the longer term, it needs to generate cash.

It is possible to have strong earnings and cash flow in the short term. This can be achieved by reducing costs to boost earnings or not investing in the business to support growth and ongoing operations. But the business won't be there for the long term with this approach.

Wendy Collie defines success as follows:

- An empowered and engaged staff who feel they are thriving and have meaning in their work
- A differentiated experience that is approachable
- An approach to providing value to customers and community through connecting them in unique ways
- A positive improvement in sales and the bottom line as a result of the aforementioned

To achieve longevity, a business must continually generate strong cash flows and EBITDA (earnings before interest, tax, depreciation, and amortization). And to do that, the business must be a good corporate citizen. If the business acts unethically, harms the environment, or goes against accepted norms, it will suffer a blow. Whether it is a permanent blow or a temporary one is a matter of the significance of the infraction and how well the business works to resolve it.

So, success is ultimately about doing the right things and having an impact. When you are doing that well, you will see financial results that are commensurate with a high-performing business.

Is your organization high-performing? I designed the following assessment (see Table 1.1) to give you insight into the areas in which your organization is doing well and those that need a little more attention. The

Table 1.1 The high-performing index

	Yes	No
Every person in your business can explain what your business is about (your purpose).		
You are constantly being asked by customers, industry associations, publications, and advisers to speak and give tours of your facility.		
Your organization's earnings are in the top 10 percent of your industry.		
Your people are constantly being sought by other businesses and they choose to stay with you.		
Your people work collaboratively across the organization to further your goals.		
You have healthy debate when making decisions, varying perspectives are shared, and a decision is made and acted on quickly.		
New products are constantly being innovated and introduced.		
Your customers are so pleased by your goods or services, they actively recommend them to others.		
You regularly share your goals and expectations, as well as how your organization is performing.		
Your expectations are high, and you know your people are capable of achieving your goals.		
Your earnings are constantly growing, and the dips mirror market swings and are not a loss of market share or declining margins.		
Your energy is high, and you are excited to go to work every day.		
You have a group of people who inspire you and who will give you frank perspectives and advice when needed.		

questions get at the concepts that will be discussed through the course of this book. The questions are designed to look at the entirety of your business and should be answered that way. Even if you don't have responsibility for the entire business, there are ways you can impact it.

If you answered "Yes" to 12 to 13, including the questions about earnings, you are doing well and outperforming. Congratulations! Undoubtedly, one of your greatest traits is continuing to learn and grow. You'll find several insights as you keep reading this book.

If you answered "Yes" to 9 to 11, including the question about earnings, you are pretty close to outperforming and have the groundwork substantially in place. There's a bit of work to do, but you are a long way down the road.

If you answered "No" to the question about earnings and have fewer than eight questions answered "Yes," the good news is you have lots of upside potential. With a bit of work, your company can outperform competitors.

If you want a more detailed version of the High-Performing Index assessment, go to my website www.heidipozzo.com/high-performing.

Why Does High-Performance Matter?

Over the last century, the largest sectors have changed significantly for the 50 largest companies. The best measure of size in 1917 was assets. Steel was by far the largest industry sector. By 1967, using market value, oil and gas was the largest sector. In both rankings, the automotive sector ranked middle of the pack. By 2017, the tech sector became the largest sector as evaluated by market size. Automotive no longer made the top 50. AT&T and General Electric were the only two companies on the list in 1917 and 2017.

In 1965, companies spent 33 years on average on the Fortune 500. By 2026, Fortune 500 tenure is expected to decline to 14 years. Eighty-eight percent of the companies in the Fortune 500 in 1955 (the first year of ranking companies) were no longer on the list in 2014, according to the American Enterprise Institute. The reason? Too much time was spent on day-to-day activities, and not enough time was spent on strategy and innovation.

To achieve longevity, companies must constantly reinvent themselves.

Those that have survived beyond the last half century are financial, food, consumer products, transportation, and appliances. They are in business models that have not been disrupted yet but have required innovations to stay relevant. The companies include JP Morgan Chase, Cigna, Colgate-Palmolive, DuPont, Boeing, Campbell Soup, General Motors, Kellogg, Procter & Gamble, John Deere, IBM, and Whirlpool.

While the Fortune 500 measures the largest companies by revenue, it is a good proxy for what is happening in business. You may be thinking many of the companies you know are much smaller than these, and the timelines don't apply. It is a mistake to dismiss these statistics outright. The length of time may be extended before disruption trickles through the industry. But make no mistake, changes that happen with the largest companies will eventually trickle through to all sizes of business.

High-performing leaders see the signs that it is time to course correct. They see the plateaus and disruptions and take the actions necessary not just to survive, but to thrive. Without that type of leadership, businesses will eventually cease to exist. We'll get to the building blocks of what they do a little bit later in this chapter.

Figure 1.1 illustrates a visual way to think about the various stages of your business.

The conditions necessary for a business to be high-performing require the right people with the right skills and the right focus. Companies must keep this in mind and adapt over time not just to stay in business, but to outperform.

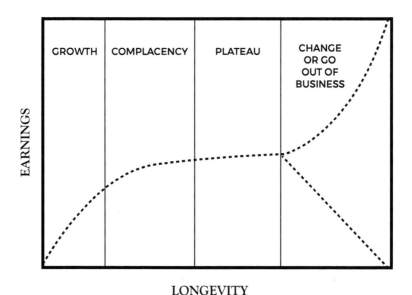

Figure 1.1 Your business lifecycle

Beyond that, working in a business that is high-performing has some benefits that you may not expect:

- Engagement is high.
- It is easy to get work done.
- People know how they fit into the business.
- Customers are delighted with their products or services.
- Investors are pleased with the return on their investment.
- The community has a robust supplier of jobs, taxes, and support.

Having the right leadership matters, because everything the business touches will be impacted by how the business is run—either positively or negatively. And having high-performing leaders makes a quantum difference.

Barriers to Outperforming

Years ago, I was working with a business that had a number of challenges. Earnings were sagging, and there was no clear focus on the business. An attempt to get back to basics and focus on operational and financial drivers was balked at by a chorus of people declaring the business was different.

But the business wasn't different. Thinking you are different and the fundamentals don't apply is an excuse for poor performance. Being different only matters when you are doing something that is propelling your business forward in a sustainable and profitable manner.

Many of the barriers to outperforming get built into businesses over time. Slowly, a lack of insight into how other businesses operate creeps in.

Day-to-day activities begin to overwhelm the ability to get out and talk to others in the industry, to customers, or to other business leaders in the area. As a result, the ability to recognize well-run companies and emerging business models diminishes, because leaders no longer have insight into what others are doing.

There are several signs that show up on the horizon and start creeping into the business before the financials are impacted. The following barometer (see Figure 1.2) will give you a pressure reading on your organization to see what is coming.

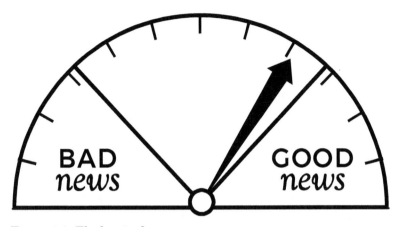

Figure 1.2 The barrier barometer

Bad News	Good News
• Top talent is leaving. • You don't think you can afford top talent. • Customer orders are declining. • You don't have an R&D budget. • Failures are punished. • People say "We are different" to explain poor performance. • Your bank is asking you a lot of questions about your customers and marketing plans. • You don't know your market share. • You don't know your productivity or earnings versus those of your competitors. • Making decisions and getting work done takes extended periods of time.	• Top talent flocks to you, and you hire them even if you don't have a job opening. • Customers are working with you collaboratively to develop new products. • Resources are dedicated to innovating. • A culture of learning is in place. • Your bank compliments you about being on top of your business and admits it wishes others were as good as you. • You know where you stand in the market versus competitors. • The pace of work and decision making is fast, and you know it.

Where is the pointer on your barometer?

The good news is that wherever you find your organization on the barometer, there are things you can do right away to move the dial. Even if you are doing well, outperforming is not a destination, it is a journey.

Everything about your business will change in the next few years, so moving forward is important to your longevity.

Complacency and Lack of Focus Always Creep In

I like the Ford story, because the company has been around for more than 100 years. And in that time, we can see what has worked and what has not. We don't just have a small slice in time. Ford has innovated, become complacent, refocused, and grown. As much as we would all like to believe that our business will not hit a rough patch, it will. And usually, it happens around a leadership change.

In 1903, Henry Ford founded The Ford Motor Company. He was a pioneer in the automotive industry. To meet growing demand for the Model T, he designed the moving assembly line. Its success led to widespread adoption. Henry Ford took another revolutionary action: He doubled the pay of his workers, laying the groundwork for a strong middle class in the United States.

After a century in business, Ford lost its way. It was 2006, and Ford was in a crisis. Market share was suffering, costs were skyrocketing, and the cycle time for new vehicle introductions was lagging behind Japanese competitors. Ford was no longer innovating. Ford had become complacent and was staring bankruptcy in the eye. The changes made by a prior leader put the company under significant strain (we'll cover this in Chapter 8). It was time for a new leader.

Alan Mulally spent his entire career up to that point at Boeing, after starting as an engineer right out of college. After being passed up twice by Boeing to ascend to the CEO role, he joined Ford as CEO on September 5, 2006.

Mulally came to Ford when it was about to post its largest loss in history. The market had not yet crashed, yet Ford's bonds were classified as junk, and there were concerns it was about to go bankrupt. Labor costs were $76/hour versus Toyota's $48/hour. Ford's brands were not doing well and required major capital infusions to become competitive again.

Within 90 days of joining Ford, Mulally raised $23.6 billion to bridge the gap to profitability. An extensive restructuring plan was put in place to reduce operating costs, shed the luxury brands that were weighing Ford down, reintroduce the flagship Taurus, and move toward

Table 1.2 Ford financial highlights

Key Statistics	Low	High
Stock price	$1.26 (November 19, 2008)	$18.79 (January 27, 2011)
Revenue	$118.3B 2009	$172.5B 2007
EBITDA	$8.2B 2008	$17.1B 2014
Net income	($14.7B) 2008	$7.2B 2013*

*2011 had the highest net income at $20.2B but had an $11.5B benefit from income taxes.
Source: Yahoo Financial for stock, ADVFN for income statement.

lighter-weight, fuel-efficient cars. All of this required intense focus on goals and collaboration to right the ship.

Over the course of his eight-year tenure as CEO, Mulally was able to restore profitability amidst the global crisis by focusing on the nine building blocks we will cover in this chapter. You can see the impact he had on the performance of the company in Table 1.2.

After Mulally's retirement, things began to stall out again. Under Mark Fields, profits and stock prices declined through his three-year tenure. Ford once again looked externally to find a transformational leader to compete in the future automobile market. It found its new leader in Jim Hackett, former CEO of Steelcase. His history of transforming both Steelcase and University of Michigan football, along with his contacts in Silicon Valley, positioned him to take the helm of Ford in May 2017.

In Ford's case, one or more of the nine key elements (outlined ahead) were lost at each point Ford saw a decline in its business. The company lost focus and fell from being a top performer. These indicators serve as good warning signs for all businesses.

Being high-performing does not occur via a mere checklist, however. It is a state of being. It is about continual growth, innovation, and focus. When it all comes together, it is a fantastic and invigorating place to be.

Your Roadmap to High-Performance

Now that we've covered what being high-performing looks like, why it is important, and what the barriers are to achieving it, we'll jump into how to achieve it.

To be high-performing, there are nine building blocks that correspond to the coming chapters:

- Finding or renewing your purpose
- Innovating to stay relevant
- Building and sustaining a high-performing team
- Identifying and engaging your following
- Keeping score and outperforming
- Setting and communicating high expectations
- Avoiding plateaus
- Being your personal best
- Identifying and enrolling personal advisers

Each one is necessary to fully achieve top-performing status and stay there. You can't skip any of these building blocks and expect to be a long-term sustainable business.

This book is organized into four parts—the first three are about your business. The fourth part is about you. As leadership and the performance of your business are intertwined, it takes you operating at your best for your business to operate at its best. Here's the overview:

- Part I: Purpose and Relevance: Why Your Business Exists and How to Evolve to Stay Relevant
- Part II: Your Team Extends Beyond the Four Walls of the Business
- Part III: Keeping Score and Reaching New Heights
- Part IV: You: Becoming a Leader Who Is a Fine-Tuned Machine

You can find a complete roadmap of the concepts and performance accelerators in Appendix A.

Remember your High-Performing Index score? Those questions relate to the building blocks that are in the chapters to come. No matter where you scored on the High-Performing Index, there will be insights ahead.

Let's get started!

PART I

Purpose and Relevance: Why Your Business Exists and How to Evolve to Stay Relevant

CHAPTER 2

Fueling Your Performance through Purpose

Mark Zuckerberg stumbled onto his company's purpose early in life. As a young boy, he created a system similar to an instant messenger system to communicate with his family. His father was a dentist and ran his business at home. Part of the house was the business, and the other part was the residence. The communication system let family members touch base throughout the day.

He had the same desire to connect with his classmates who lived in the next town, across the bridge. He wasn't yet able to drive, and they were too far away to spend time with after school, so they used AOL Instant Messenger to communicate. Not being able to spend time together was foundational in forming his views about connecting and communities.

The early version of Facebook was developed while Zuckerberg was at Harvard. He wanted to create a platform for his classmates to connect. It caught on so quickly that he rolled it out to one university after another. Upon taking a leave from Harvard to scale his business, it became clear that he was on to something. So, he left Harvard and looked forward to growing what is now one of the world's most valuable companies.

Zuckerberg was clear about Facebook's purpose—to connect people. As he continued to look at why people wanted to connect and what resonated with them, he recognized that people wanted to be part of a community. He revised Facebook's purpose to reflect people's desire to build communities. The purpose-driven focus of the business has been so powerful that Facebook topped two billion monthly users by mid-2017.

Facebook was founded in 2004. In the space of 13 years, it was able to go from nothing to connecting a little more than 25 percent of the world's population. That is the power of purpose.

Like Zuckerberg, Blake Mycoskie, founder of TOMS, had a clear purpose. Only it took him a bit longer to find it.

Mycoskie found his inspiration while on vacation in Argentina. Kids couldn't go to school because shoes were required and many didn't have them. Those who did have shoes were wearing the same type of shoe: a plain, utilitarian slip-on made with canvas.

What if he could start a business that supported the local economy while introducing the "one for one" concept into business? For each shoe purchased, one would be given away to a child in need (one for one). He extended his stay in Argentina to get contracts with local shoemakers to launch his business.

When he returned to California, his sister served as a sounding board for his new business. It quickly became clear that the purpose of the company was about one for one. His original marketing focused on the price point and utility. Helping kids get shoes was not in the original marketing. He connected the purpose with the customer through marketing by introducing the "one for one" concept, and that is when the message started resonating. Tomorrow's Shoes was born. With a name too long to fit on a shoe, it was shortened to TOMS.

The message resonated so clearly with his target audience that the company grew rapidly from its 2006 start. Over the course of a decade, they gave away more than 70 million shoes. The company's revenues were estimated to be $500 million in 2016. Mycoskie sold half of the company to Bain Capital in 2014, with an estimated valuation of $625 million.

What started out as a purpose-driven company became a profitable business. As it scaled, the cost of producing the shoes rapidly declined, allowing the company to serve a social purpose while being profitable. In addition to providing shoes, it has also funded cataract surgeries—to give people their vision—and provided safe drinking water. TOMS became so successful, it spawned an entire industry of one for one–focused products and companies.

Zuckerberg and Mycoskie were both able to identify a need in the market and build a business that centered around purpose. It was the clarity of that purpose that resonated with customers and allowed the businesses to scale rapidly.

People want to be part of a community. They want to be associated with your business, because of how they feel when they interact with it, not because of facts and data. Facebook's and TOMS' journey highlights the five performance accelerators I've identified as key. Each of these concepts will help you clarify what you are about.

Pozzo Performance Accelerators:

1. Your purpose needs to be clear and unambiguous.
2. Your purpose should be at the center of everything you do.
3. Your purpose needs to resonate with customers.
4. Your employees should share a passion for your purpose.
5. Your profit and purpose don't need to be at odds.

In this chapter, we'll build out each of the five concepts and provide some helpful tools to introduce these concepts into your organization or refine your thinking if you already have a good start. This chapter is focused on the purpose of your business. As such, when we discuss your purpose, you should be thinking in the context of your business.

Performance Accelerator 1: Your Purpose Needs to Be Clear and Unambiguous

Knowing the purpose of your company seems easy and obvious. And for some, it is. They just know in their bones what the business is about, and it shows in all the actions they take. They can tell you in one sentence what the business is about, and you get it. Clarity.

For others, it takes a while to figure out the purpose. The conversation may be long and rambling—a sign that clarity does not yet exist. Whether finding it easily or over time, clarity is essential. Your purpose needs to be clear and unambiguous because it influences the customers you attract, the people who want to be part of your company, and the way work happens every day.

Many founders are clear about the purpose of their businesses when they start. It is what attracts others to the business. It is compelling; yet, as people change and the years go by, the purpose can become diluted. That is why it is important to periodically check in on whether the purpose of your business is still clear and compelling.

You will get instant feedback about the clarity of your purpose and how well it is resonating with others. By sharing your purpose, you are explicitly telling people what to expect when doing business with your organization. And by doing so, you will learn whether people understand your purpose.

Clearly, there is a benefit to knowing your purpose. So, how do you find yours? There are five steps that can help you find your purpose. They involve writing down what is important, seeking internal and external feedback, understanding your capabilities, and knowing where you stack up against competitors.

As you read through this section, use the guide in Table 2.1 to gain clarity on your purpose.

Wendy Collie understands the importance of being clear and unambiguous about purpose.

When describing the importance of clearly stating the purpose of a business, she stresses that it isn't just necessary to clearly state what the purpose is; it must also be intentional, vividly described, and shared broadly across the organization. If any of these aspects are missing, people will fill in their own gaps.

Her litmus test at New Seasons was to talk to people at all levels and hear what they knew about the company and its purpose, why the business existed, and so on. If the individuals didn't understand, the communication by leadership wasn't successful.

With the purpose in mind, New Seasons started their communication and common purpose work on day one of orientation. The history, purpose, mission of the company, and values were shared during orientation to entrench people up front. A lot of storytelling occurred, which helps

Table 2.1 *Finding or renewing your purpose*

What is it about your business that is important and meaningful?
Why is it important?
Why do your customers and investors do business with you?
Why do your suppliers or partners do business with you?
What do you do well (your capabilities)?
What sets you apart from your competitors?

bring the company to life by creating emotional attachments and excitement. Then everything else was taught.

Wherever you are in the organization, by understanding the purpose and bringing it to life, you can have an impact. If the purpose isn't clear to you, it isn't clear to others. Many of the following steps are within your reach.

Write Down What Is Important and Why

Nothing brings more focus than writing something down. You may start with a blank sheet of paper and struggle to get words on the paper. Or maybe the words come easily, and the paper fills rapidly. Either way, getting the words on paper makes them real and creates a focus that just talking or thinking doesn't do.

The words that describe your purpose should ultimately be clear and concise. Can they be boiled down to one or two sentences? If your purpose is longer than that, the possibility of a misunderstanding becomes higher. People start to tune out or become confused.

Indicating why your purpose is important can bring additional clarity. In many cases, the purpose may be obvious. In other cases, it may not. By writing down why your organization is in business, revisions to the purpose may be necessary to ensure the intention of the why is reflected in the purpose itself.

As one of the largest employers in the community, Longview's fate had a significant impact on the community. At the time I joined the business in 2007, it was not operating well, and many in the community feared it would be shut down. Creating a long-term, sustainable business was important to the future of the community. That perspective was written down and displayed throughout the company.

Ask Key Stakeholders Who Pay You

The most insightful perspectives about your business may come from people who do business with you.

From a customer perspective, you will hear what your business does well and why customers keep coming back. Equally important is hearing from former customers or those you would like to do business with but don't. Their perspectives may tell you if there is a gap between what you believe you are delivering and what others believe you are delivering. It will tell you if you are living up to your purpose.

Why do your customers buy from you and not your competitors? Price is sometimes the answer, but not always. Your customers buy from you for some set of reasons. Maybe you are easy to do business with. Maybe your purpose is aligned with theirs. The reason for their purchases is typically deliberate.

For example, when I was at Longview, we reached out to customers to understand why they bought from us. For some, it was about the quality of the product and timeliness of delivery. And for others, it was about the relationship and the quality—the close working relationship that resulted in products that were fit for purpose and worked well for both parties.

Similarly, your investors put money into your company for a specific reason. Some may want a specific return. Others may be interested in activities your company is engaged in. For others, it may be about the purpose of your company. Understanding why they are investing in you and ensuring that you are on the same page is important.

Each of these perspectives will give you insight about why people and organizations spend money with you. Whether that perspective is how you perceive your purpose or not will serve to either refine what your purpose is or provide feedback on the need to change how you operate to align perception with your intended purpose.

Ask Key Stakeholders Who You Pay

At times, experiences can be significantly different for those who are on the receiving end of the dollar. High-performing organizations do not typically distinguish treatment of people and companies on the basis of the dollar flow. This area is one that will tell you how well your purpose and values are showing up every day.

People who work in your organization have a unique perspective. They may or may not understand what you are trying to accomplish, your purpose. Formal methods of feedback include engagement surveys. Informal methods can include walking around and having conversations.

Unless you have a high degree of trust, it is unlikely you will get a full perspective through informal methods. And you really need your people's perspective. Beyond how well they understand your purpose, you also want to know if you are living it. If that trust isn't there today, you'll need a neutral third party to have these conversations and begin building trust.

Your suppliers are also a wealth of information on what you do well. Your interactions and how easy or hard it is for your suppliers to do business with you will say a lot about your purpose. Every interaction is an opportunity to display your purpose and values. Do you partner and work collaboratively with your suppliers, or do you treat them poorly? If you do this well, you'll find they will provide you with connections to new business as well.

Throughout my career, the one theme that has been consistent is customers value when you understand their businesses and deliver a product or service they value. At Ernst & Young, for example, clients valued audit teams that understood their business and targeted the audit appropriately. What do your customers value? How can you deliver based on what they value?

The perspective of those you pay is typically very insightful. Their insights may be delightful and something not previously considered—or may be a different take on what you do well and why you exist. You may get a very different perspective from the people and organizations you pay—maybe even one that is not good. In any case, this feedback will help shape your purpose and next steps.

Outline Your Capabilities and Their Impact

Part of defining your purpose is knowing what your organization does well—its capabilities. Maybe you can produce a product faster than anyone out there. Or you have outstanding customer service. List all the capabilities of your organization that set it apart or are critical to its operations and confirm that they are indeed the key capabilities.

Your organization's capabilities should naturally fit with the intended purpose. For example, let's say your business makes seatbelts. Seatbelts save lives (your purpose). If your capabilities include creating no defects/high quality and having the ability to meet customer demand, your capabilities support your purpose. But if you have high defects/failure rate in accidents and you can't satisfy customer demand, your capabilities may not be supporting your purpose (saving lives).

If your capabilities and purpose are not quite aligned, it is time to figure out which needs adjusting—the purpose or the capabilities.

Describe What Sets You Apart from Your Competitors

You do things well in your business. So do your competitors. Do you know what you do well and how that stacks up against what your competitors do? Getting an internal perspective from people within your business about what your business does well and its shortcomings versus the strengths and weaknesses of each competitor is important. Having an external perspective from people outside your business on how you and your competitors stack up is critical.

External perspectives are available from many sources. Industry publications showing financial performance may be available by submitting data on your business or paying a fee. Depending on how sensitive the information is, you may get a customized report that shows your information specifically and that of the rest of the industry combined. Banks, auditors, insurance companies, and consultants also have perspectives and varying levels of industry analysis on the basis of what they see in doing business with others. The information you receive from these sources may be informal to formal, with confidentiality considered.

At Longview, we had access to certain raw materials (wood chips from slow growing trees) that were not available in other places around the United States, or the world. Combined with equipment in the facility, we could make products that only one or two others in the world could make. Re-creating the combination of the two was cost prohibitive, creating a natural barrier in certain areas.

Linfield College has a similar advantage, situated in the heart of the Willamette Valley. President Tom Hellie was able to leverage this distinguishing factor in its wine program, as the only college in the United States with a program focused on the soft skills necessary to run a successful winery. The degree was a minor and recently became a major.

Linfield's nursing program is the oldest in the state of Oregon—and unusual in that it emphasizes a very rich and interdisciplinary liberal arts set of requirements. As a result, the students have strong communication skills and the ability to think on their feet, resulting in many becoming head nurses.

Understanding what sets you apart from your competitors ultimately gets to purpose. The reason why customers buy from you versus your competitors should be a reflection of your purpose.

Performance Accelerator 2: Your Purpose Should Be at the Center of Everything You Do

One way to think about the purpose being at the center of your business is to think about it in terms of the solar system as depicted in Figure 2.1. Your purpose would be like the sun; its gravitational pull keeps all of your stakeholders in your orbit. The light and warmth cause all in your solar system to grow and flourish.

The purpose of an organization should be stable and rarely change. The tactics may change frequently. It is critical for leaders to be consistent in how they discuss the purpose of the organization internally

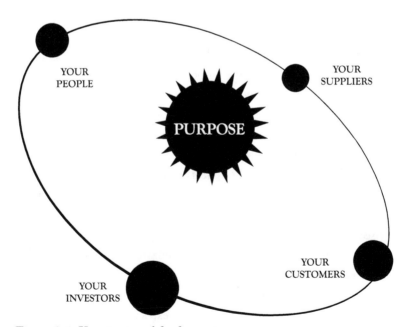

Figure 2.1 Your purposeful solar system

and externally. Whether it is about building communities or providing solutions that make everyday life easier, pick your favorite purpose, and that purpose should be front and center of everything. The actions being taken by the organization should support the purpose and be easy to understand.

By being clear and consistent about your organization's purpose, every person in the organization should know how his or her actions impact the larger organization and purpose. And if they don't know, asking for clarification is not only acceptable, it is expected.

In a purpose-driven organization, the purpose should be discussed on a regular, if not daily, basis. Conversations should happen as part of sales meetings, business reviews, employee communications, and so on. How the purpose is discussed should be consistent each time it is discussed. By discussing the purpose frequently, the message will be reinforced—as long as it is consistent.

People look to leadership to confirm whether the organization is really about what it says it is about. People will look to leadership for clues in words and actions of the real purpose. If actions are consistent with words, the authenticity of the purpose and trust in the organization are reinforced. Consistency in communication and actions builds trust.

But it isn't just about leaders. People at all levels of the organization should act consistently with the purpose of the organization. Customers expect the experience that was promised by the organization through its purpose. At the end of the day, engaged employees tend to deliver on the stated purpose of the organization. They walk the talk.

Sharing your purpose doesn't need to be complicated. It can be done through talks with local business or industry groups, conversations one-on-one, marketing materials, your website, articles in the newspaper, and so on. However you choose to tell everyone, your purpose should be consistent.

By sharing the purpose of your organization broadly, you'll find that a natural attraction is beginning to develop. Customers who share your sense of purpose become attracted to you. So do employees. It tells stakeholders what kind of experience to expect from you. It sets the foundation for everything you do.

Performance Accelerator 3: Your Purpose Needs to Resonate with Customers

Your purpose signals to customers what you are about and how you will engage with them, attracting the right customers to you. Some customers will buy on price, but as soon as a lower price pops up somewhere else, they will move away from you just as fast as they came to you. From a long-term perspective, this is not the right customer with whom to build a business that outperforms.

Just as with Facebook and TOMS, meeting the needs of your customers in a way that really resonates will attract customers quickly and cause them to stay. You are not just meeting a need but doing it in a way that connects your business with theirs. You are offering something that is distinct from those of your competitors.

In being clear about your purpose and sticking to it, you also indicate to customers what you will do and what you won't do. For example, CVS stopped selling cigarettes and tobacco products in 2014, prompted by its purpose to focus on the health of its customers. While it lost $2 billion in annual sales, it felt it was the right thing to do. By making this decision, it was able to focus more on other pharmacy and medical services that made up for the loss in tobacco.

At Linfield, students value the 11:1 student-to-faculty ratio. The small size of the college allows for close relationships that are transformative to the students. The faculty has the ability to mentor and inspire the students, and the students recognize it.

You will always hear commentary from people who do not buy into your purpose. It is important to ignore that commentary. Don't try to serve everyone. Listen only to your customers or former customers to check that you aren't drifting off your purpose.

Performance Accelerator 4: Your Employees Should Share a Passion for Your Purpose

Companies are looking for more from their people than just the technical skills necessary to complete a job. They are increasingly focused on hiring for fit. They are looking for alignment between the values of the person and the values of the company. This requires the individual to clearly understand what is important to them. It also requires the company to know what it stands for.

Finding the source of passion in your people and making sure it aligns with the purpose of your company is critical. If employees really believe in what they are doing, it shows up as discretionary effort—that intangible that causes people to pay a little more attention and put a little more effort or passion into what they are doing. And it shows. Quality is typically higher, the customer experience is better, and employee engagement is higher.

Performance Accelerator 5: Your Profit and Purpose Don't Need to Be at Odds

People want to work for companies that are about more than just making money. They want to have a positive impact on their customers and their communities. They want to make a difference. By focusing on purpose, people become more engaged. While this is true for everyone, it is especially important for the generations that are entering the workforce today.

Deloitte found that businesses that focus on purpose rather than profits tended to have higher anticipated growth potential and attract more capital as outlined in its research "Culture of Purpose—Building Business Confidence; Driving Growth 2014 Core Beliefs & Culture Survey."

In a 2012 study titled, "How Employee Engagement Drives Growth," Gallup found organizations with high employee engagement had 21 percent higher productivity and 22 percent higher profits than companies with actively disengaged employees. According to Jim Harter of Gallup, "Engaged workers . . . have bought into what the organization is about and are trying to make a difference. This is why they're usually the most productive workers."

Businesses don't attract and retain the best people through money. While money is a factor in deciding where to work, it is only a hurdle. In other words, if you aren't offering enough to make the job interesting, people won't consider it. But if you are, it is only a starting point, after which many other factors come into play. Again, people want to make a difference, so the job must be one with a purpose that is about more than just making money.

Given the importance of purpose in engaging employees and helping a business to thrive, you need to outline the purpose of the organization—simply, clearly, and in a way that creates an emotional connection. Purpose is about more than statistics and discrete goals. It is the way you feel when you know things are better off because you were involved. And when the people within the company are excited and engaged internally, it will reflect well in all their external interactions.

Your Actions

Your purpose is the guiding light for your organization. There is a direct correlation between having a purpose, having engaged people in the organization, and delivering the expected results. Focusing on a purpose is subtly different from focusing on an outcome. By focusing on doing the right thing based on the purpose, people are bought in. They want to make a difference. And the by-product or outcome is delivering the expected experience—with higher productivity and earnings.

As you reflect on this chapter, consider how strongly your purpose is resonating with people. No matter where you are in your organization, you can have an impact. If your purpose is clear, living your company's purpose will reinforce it with everyone you interact with. If it is not, engaging with senior leadership and asking questions can highlight a gap or clarify your understanding. Either way, if you aren't clear, others probably aren't either. The following are actions and questions necessary to ensure your purpose is clear and unambiguous:

- Complete the guide to finding or renewing your purpose.
- Talk to the people in your solar system and get their perspective on your purpose. Is it what you expected?
- Are your capabilities aligned with your purpose?
- What other gaps do you need to close after reading this chapter, and what resources do you need to close them?

CHAPTER 3

Creativity, Questions, and Failure

Supercharging Innovation

When was the last time you went to Blockbuster to rent a movie? It used to be a weekend ritual for many families: Hop into the car and drive to the closest video rental store. Each family member would wander down a favorite aisle. The new releases would be reviewed, as would the movies on the list that hadn't yet been seen. A little give-and-take occurred to decide which one or two would be rented—then off home to a fun evening or weekend.

Fast forward to today. No longer do you hop into a car to decide which movie to rent. It is as easy as picking up a remote to your TV or looking at your device of preference and choosing your movie through a streaming service.

How did we get there? You can thank a $40 late fee for inspiring Reed Hastings to develop Netflix. Some say the story is fiction. In any case, Hastings knew that a significant portion of the revenues came from late fees. He and his partner, Marc Randolph, set out to change the way people viewed movies by founding Netflix in 1997.

Netflix began as a single rental service by sending DVDs through the mail to customers, moving quickly to a subscription service based on customer feedback. The long-term goal was to provide streaming services, hence the name Netflix. With a tech background, the founders knew the Internet would be capable of streaming, but it would be a decade until the bandwidth was there. As the capabilities of the Internet advanced, Netflix was able to begin streaming in 2007. At that point, it had grown from one million customers in 2003 to 7.5 million customers in 2007.

With the shift in its model from mailing DVDs to streaming services, the opportunities to expand quickly opened. Netflix began its international expansion in 2011—and producing its own content in 2013 with *House of Cards*. These moves exponentially grew the number of subscribers to nearly 94 million by the end of 2016.

Hastings is one of the few CEOs who have been able to scale from a start-up to a public company and effectively guide the business through its growth. So, how did the ideas come about to innovate through this period? Look everywhere for inspiration, and there are no new business models, only delivery mechanisms.

Hastings thought about the life span of business models and when major changes would disrupt it. But he wasn't the first to do so. The horse was a dominant form of transportation for 5,000 years. Innovations were made to make transportation more efficient and comfortable, such as the introduction of the saddle and the carriage. The automobile with an internal combustion engine was introduced in the late 1800s, disrupting the horse as the dominant form of transportation.

Some may say the automobile became an entirely new business model. But there is another way to look at it. People are still being transported; the only thing that has changed is *how.* When you consider new ways of transporting people rather than fixating on how they have been transported, it opens the possibilities of where to look for inspiration on how to innovate.

Brian Chesky, co-founder of Airbnb, looked to *Snow White and the Seven Dwarfs* for inspiration at a critical juncture. He realized after reading a biography of Walt Disney that Disney was at a similar juncture when the decision was made to develop a full-length animated feature film, something that had never been done. It was a bet-the-farm decision. But it was one that paid off. The creators used storyboards to communicate the vision and create the story.

Chesky brought that process into Airbnb. The team storyboarded the guest process, the host process, and the hiring process. In doing so, it required the team to understand what guests and hosts feel, who they are, and what they like. They had to really understand each of their stakeholders.

The team soon realized that most of the Airbnb experience was offline, in the homes. That led to the realization that the website was not the center of the experience. Technology should support the experience, not be the experience. As a result, mobile became more of a focus. By focusing on the experience, the mobile technology would support people wherever they happened to be—especially if they just found a place that they wanted to stay while wandering around.

The process of storyboarding allowed Airbnb to understand the experience, and not just look at it as a process devoid of people. Moving to a mobile platform allowed for a connection between online, offline, and the people involved. Netflix and Airbnb highlight my three performance accelerators related to innovation.

Pozzo Performance Accelerators:

1. Disruptive innovation comes from a friction point that completely changes the way a product or service is delivered.
2. When a new business model/method of delivery has been established, innovation becomes incremental and focused on making things better.
3. Your culture needs to reward thoughtful experiments and idea generation in order to innovate.

Underlying these concepts is the understanding of how long the business model will last. For example, automobiles disrupted horses as the major form of transporting humans. Automobiles have existed for nearly a century and a half, with no replacement on the horizon. Autonomous vehicles and ridesharing is on the rise and will eventually impact how automobiles are sold and who owns them. It is the intersection of two different ideas that have not been put together before that will disrupt any existing business model. In this case, it is technology and automobiles. Understanding how long the current model will exist informs how much to spend on disruptive innovation versus incremental innovation. While you may not know a business model is ending years before it does, it is important to watch for it.

Performance Accelerator 1: Disruptive Innovation Comes from a Friction Point That Completely Changes the Way a Product or Service Is Delivered

In the 1700s, newspaper printers were frequently also postmasters. There was no federal system in what is now the United States. Rather, each city had its own postal system that enabled the postmasters to gather and deliver news. The postmaster had the sole discretion on which newspapers could be delivered without a fee, or delivered at all.

Benjamin Franklin owned a newspaper in Philadelphia, but found this paper was barred from delivery by the postmaster/owner of a rival paper. Eventually, Franklin became joint postmaster general of America under British rule. In this capacity, Franklin abolished the ability of a postmaster to ban delivery of newspapers, sped up delivery times, mapped the postal routes, and established the penny post, wherein mail would be delivered for a penny.

The Continental Congress appointed Franklin as the first postmaster general of what would eventually become the United States Postal Service.

It is hard to imagine today that a letter back then took weeks to travel 100 miles, roads between cities were not well marked, and mail was dropped at a tavern, inn, or coffee house that served as a post office. In those days, you may not even know that a piece of mail was waiting for you.

Franklin saw the challenges not only in sharing content—the news—due to barriers, but also the ineffectiveness of the platform for getting it to people. He saw the friction point for people and revolutionized how the postal system worked in the United States.

Fast forward to today. Technology has completely changed the way content is shared. Depending upon the research or poll you read, somewhere around two-thirds of adults in the United States get their news online through websites, apps, or social media.

Communication between people has changed dramatically as well. The advent of the telephone, e-mail, and texting has caused a decline of letters mailed through the postal service.

The desire to share content and communicate with others hasn't changed since the 1700s. The manner in which we do so has changed radically, given changing platforms and friction points.

If you look at the newspaper industry, you'll see a dramatic shift in the way content is shared. While the first newspaper can be traced back to 59 BC in Rome, regular production of news didn't start until the 1600s. The newspaper industry has lasted for 400 years. Print newspaper is a mature industry and has been on the decline for years. While the newspaper industry is not completely extinct, print circulation is down by nearly half versus its peak in the 1970s and 1980s. Online consumption of news is taking the place of print.

So, how do you know when your platform is about to change?

Disruption happens at the intersection of technology and high friction. When it is hard and expensive to make a product, or customers have to spend more money to receive it, there will be a disruption.

When a disruption is missed or is not initiated by the company that should initiate it, it is because the company was too inwardly focused and broad perspectives were not employed. For example, do you think about the following?

- Newspapers or sharing news and content: *Why didn't newspaper owners start social media companies?*
- Stores or selling goods: *Why did Sears with its catalog platform miss becoming Amazon?*

By reframing how you look at your business, you are less likely to miss a disruption.

The Disruption-Spotting Capabilities Questionnaire

Questions you should be asking:

- Are my customers happy with my product or service, or do they constantly think, "There must be a better way?"
- Is there technology on the horizon that over the next few years will enable a major leap in the business?
- How am I pushing the boundaries on what is possible?
- Am I making enough time to think about what is next?

- What are the thought leaders in my industry or adjacent industries looking at?
- How long will the business model/platform last?
- Who can I get to know in other industries to take inspiration from?
- Do I have the right team in place to spot disruption?
- What are the curious people looking at?

You are in trouble if you say or act on the following:

- We are different because . . . (to explain poor performance and dismiss why a successful approach widely used in other industries won't work)
- We adhere to industry norms . . .
- We are limited by . . .
- We can't afford . . .

By spotting the impending disruptive innovation coming your way, you can get in front of it and take the lead in transforming your industry. Disruptive changes typically come at the intersection of two ideas that have not been put together before. To make this leap, you will need people from outside of your industry to work with people from inside it.

The question you will need to resolve is whether you put the initial, typically large, investment in the disruptive idea, or whether you become a fast follower and mobilize resources quickly when the disruptive idea begins to stick.

Mitzi Perdue used this approach in finding a different way to farm rice in California. She was reading an anthropological article about Vietnam. At the time, there were some very prosperous villages and others that were not.

At the crux was a farming secret that was not shared with women. The concern was that women would marry and take the farming secret to other villages. The secret was how to apply an aquatic plant called Azolla to crops. It was part fern and part algae.

Mitzi, being a rice farmer, started researching the issue and found the biggest constraint to growing big, healthy plants was nitrogen. And

Azolla would both inhibit weeds from growing and nitrogenize the soil. But it had never been used in the United States. It worked in Vietnam, given the acidic conditions and jungle environment.

Undeterred, Mitzi reached out to contacts at UC Davis and a farmer in the area who knew weeds. In bringing them together, they found a solution to adapting the plant to the United States. And very quickly, they were using Azolla on Mitzi's 12 farms.

It looked like pond scum when applied and almost totally blocked the light, inhibiting competing weeds from growing. She found an herbicide and a fertilizer in the plant.

Mitzi's father always told her that one good idea could change your life. He encouraged her to put herself in the way of getting new ideas. Little did she know that reading an anthropological article about Vietnam would lead her to making a breakthrough approach to rice farming in the United States.

Performance Accelerator 2: When a New Business Model/Method of Delivery Has Been Established, Innovation Becomes Incremental and Focused on Making Things Better

The smartphone has been in the marketplace for well over a decade now. While you could argue it has been around longer than that in places such as Japan, the widespread adoption didn't happen in the United States until the first iPhone rolled out in 2007. While there are thoughts of what could replace the smartphone, they have not yet materialized given technological challenges. A disruption has not happened, so the platform is, therefore, intact for the near term.

Your business will be overtaken by competitors that are innovating if you sit idle. The pace of change today dictates that regular improvements be made.

Over the years, a number of improvements have been made to smartphones. Battery life, touch screens, quality of photographs, texting, apps, and GPS are just a few of the many improvements. These innovations are not disruptive. They are incremental. Today, businesses should be thinking about replacing their entire product or service portfolio every

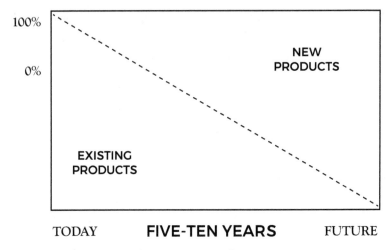

Figure 3.1 Incremental innovation accelerator

5 to 10 years. It could be a little shorter or longer on the basis of the industry. Figure 3.1 outlines how to think about it.

Here are three ways to develop incremental innovations:

Visit Your Customers' Operations to See How Your Products or Services Are Used

You will gain tremendous insight by seeing how your products or services are used by your customers. Nothing can replace going to their place of business to see how their process works and where your products fit in.

You should have a team of people regularly visiting your customers' facilities. The team should include sales and operations leads. Your salespeople know the customer and the market. Your operations people can see the product possibilities and how to make them work. They can take ideas and visualize how the products can be produced with existing equipment or necessary improvements.

As your team walks through your customers' operations, think about how you can make customers' lives easier. Ask where the bottlenecks are, what slows them down, or what would make their business even better. By doing this, you will discover the innovations your customer isn't even thinking about that you can offer them.

Ask Your Customers What They Value

When was the last time you asked your customers what they value? By asking what they value, you will find a wide range of perspectives, and not just how your products are working. Take time to understand their long-term plans and how they are innovating. During these conversations, you will hear about pain points and opportunities. These conversations help guide you to finding a win–win situation. You will know when you find the win-win, because it is valuable to both companies. And it will be the key to your next innovation.

Discover What Makes You Unique and Distinctive

Apple is well-known for having new and innovative products. You see them everywhere, and people line up to get the latest versions as soon as they are released. Preorders are placed months ahead of time. Apple creates a perception in the marketplace that its devices are much more user friendly than those of its competitors. Its customers are loyal and pay for the value they perceive in the distinctive products.

What makes your company or products unique and distinctive? It may be that you have access to raw materials that others may not. Maybe your geographic location gives you an advantage. Maybe you have an asset base that serves as a barrier to entry. Maybe it is your customer service. Being clear about what makes you and your products unique and distinctive is critical. By focusing on the unique and distinctive side of your business, you will be able to innovate and keep your customers excited about doing business with you.

Performance Accelerator 3: Your Culture Needs to Reward Thoughtful Experiments and Idea Generation in Order to Innovate

Steve Jobs was known for his tough demeanor as a leader at Apple. When asked what his proudest product achievement was, his response was unexpected. He was most proud of building a team that could innovate.

Culture and innovation work hand in hand. In building his teams at the Portland Art Museum, Brian Ferriso places a strong emphasis on culture.

His belief is that if he develops a demographically and generationally representative team, innovative ideas will emerge from within the culture.

Leadership sets the tone of what is acceptable and what is not. It shapes the culture. The culture around innovation can be one of the most delicate areas. To innovate, people must look outward and try different things that will ultimately fail. They need to think broadly and look in other areas for inspiration. Not every innovation will work out. But, a lot will be learned from trying, learning, and refining.

There are four necessary aspects to having a culture of innovation as outlined in Table 3.1.

Table 3.1 Culture of innovation indicator

	Yes	No
1. Do you have spaces that are conducive to innovation?		
2. Is your space designed such that people see each other and interact?		
3. Does your culture view failure as a learning experience?		
4. Do you have a way to focus your innovative capabilities?		

How are you stacking up? Would your people agree with your assessment? Let's take a deeper look at what the aforementioned aspects actually look like.

Create Spaces That Are Conducive to Innovation

Have you ever tried to sit in a small room devoid of any sensory input and then tried to think creatively? It is really hard. Inspiration can come through pretty settings, the outdoors, physical activity, music, paintings, or books. Companies such as Microsoft have recognized this and started experimenting with creative spaces such as tree houses. They have realized that people spend most of their time inside and need an environment conducive to generating ideas.

Conducive environments vary widely by individual. Some people enjoy the hustle and bustle of an active environment. Others need quiet and solitary environments. Putting an introvert in a high-activity space won't work well. Understanding the needs of your people is critical to getting the environment right, so ask them what they value.

People Need to Connect With Others Face-to-Face

Innovations come from solving unmet needs. People with the ideas need to meet with those who have unmet needs, and with people who can design the product or service. Connecting with people with different perspectives is necessary to finding the areas of opportunity. Steve Jobs understood this and designed spaces at Pixar and Apple that caused people to cross paths and meet regularly.

Failure Is Learning

People learn from trying and failing. The more often they try things, the better they get at succeeding. They can tell more quickly what resonates with customers. They build in mechanisms to test ideas without negatively impacting customers. More importantly, they are able to move more quickly than others, because they know what customers want and how to accomplish it. Publicly celebrate well-thought-through ideas that didn't work, and learn from what held the idea back from being successful. Encourage people to share their stories of failure.

Jim Hackett views failure as important to success. In drilling exploration wells, his company failed all the time. But what he didn't want to do was fail in the same way. If they failed in a different way than the competition, his company would get better faster and outperform their competition. With a failure culture, analyzing and learning from the failure is very powerful. It reduces risk and allows you to take more risks at the same time.

Develop Mechanisms for Focusing Innovation

When Steve Jobs returned to Apple, he found there were too many products and activities going on. The people were spread too thin and trying to do too much. He reeled back the number of products that were under development and put a process in place to balance innovation with focus. As a result, the team was able to focus on completing the products under development.

Like Jobs, Linfield College focuses innovation through an incubator called the Linfield Center for the Northwest. Funds are provided to study issues or points of interest in the area. The wine studies program is an example of a successful innovation that grew out of the incubator.

Your Actions

To understand where you should focus your efforts, you need to understand how long your business model will be in place. While you won't always know for sure when a disruption will arise, if you add disruption-spotting capabilities addressed in Performance Accelerator 1, you will be well positioned.

If there are decades of life in your business, your attention is best spent on incremental change. On the other hand, if your business model life span is nearing the end, you will need to spend time on both disruptive and incremental innovation. The culture you establish and foster will determine how successful you are in innovating.

In closing out this chapter, ask yourself the following questions:

- How much longer will your business model exist?
- What capabilities do you need to build in to spot disruption?
- What resources have you dedicated to developing incremental innovations?
- What is your product pipeline that represents your incremental innovations?
- What do you need to put into place to strengthen your culture of innovation?
- How are you encouraging people to share nutty ideas and share failures?
- What other gaps do you need to close after reading this chapter, and what resources do you need to close them?

PART II

Your Team Extends Beyond the Four Walls of the Business

CHAPTER 4

Dating, Proposing, and Marrying

The Alchemy of a Team

Do you know anyone who went to speed dating then straight to the chapel to get married? Probably not. But many times, the hiring process looks this way. And for key people in the business who set the tone and pace of the organization, getting the right people is critical.

Businesses should think about hiring people as getting married. That means you should take your time to make sure there is a fit in values, expectations, and goals; look past the shiny exterior to make sure there is a solid foundation. Attracting and retaining the right people will make or break the organization. The right people will lift the organization to new heights. The wrong people will drag it down.

Jim Hackett spent his career building high-performing teams. Like many leaders, he refined his perspectives over the years. In building a team today, he places great weight on having similar values, having different strengths, and being dependable and trustworthy. But more than that, his team members must be good communicators, good team players, and accountable.

Over the course of his career, he had the opportunity to work with many people—people who he knew and trusted. He knew their values and how they operated. And they were different from him. They thought differently, and as a team, complemented each other.

As he became CEO of Anadarko in 2003, his challenge was not to replace the entire team and bring in people he knew from his past. Rather, he wanted to establish trust and be fair to the people who were there. And so began a six-month mutual evaluation period.

With different viewpoints being crucial to having strong results, he asked people who had worked with him before to exaggerate their first honest disagreement. He wanted people to know that having a professional disagreement and working through it in the open is critical to getting to the best outcome. And that leads to a culture where all can voice their opinions.

Throughout the six months, the strategy was laid out, and two levels of management sat through weekly meetings. During this time, it became clear to Jim and the team who was aligned with the values and strategy of the organization. It was important that each position wasn't just a job, but a passion and a purpose.

During his tenure at Anadarko, the stock price went from the low $20 per share to mid-$80 per share when he announced his retirement. The team he constructed was able to execute a strategy to drive growth and value.

Stephen Babson at Endeavour Capital takes a similar approach. When looking at the teams in the businesses he is considering for purchase, he assesses if the team "self identifies" as a team. Meaning, they are not a mere group of individuals who happen to work at the same place. All of the senior leaders acknowledge that they are part of a team that works together to achieve common goals. Each has a sense of responsibility to carry one's own weight and a sense of responsibility for the others on the team. They also recognize their CEO as an effective leader.

Effective teams run with growth opportunities more effectively. Members of these teams also know each other well and know how their teammates will perform; they are predictable. And you really see their effectiveness when the market turns south. High-performing teams will excel in adverse situations.

Given this focus on team and leadership, Stephen and Endeavour have developed a strong track record in the private-equity space in the Pacific Northwest.

I've found these perspectives fundamental to being on a high-performing team. A key differentiator has been obtaining clarity about what needs to be done, how decisions are made, and who owns each area of business. In building teams, spending a lot of time up front to get clear on expectations allows each member to operate with a common platform and accelerate progress.

Working with several private-equity firms, one of the most notable distinctions in building a team has been the pace of work. It's not about just doing more in less time. It is about setting a pace and accomplishing objectives quickly. This approach requires prioritization of high-impact items and elimination of work that does not add value.

In high-performing teams, people know what to expect of each other, know when they need to talk, and move quickly to get results. Getting the team together and working effectively takes a concerted effort. Here's what it takes.

Pozzo Performance Accelerators:

1. Acquire the right skills and capabilities, and avoid critical mistakes.
2. Drive the business with top talent—in the right place.
3. Find the balance of people who have been in the organization and people new to the organization.
4. Create a direct line of sight for each person to the overarching goals.
5. Bust through resistance and conflict.
6. Get rid of friction points that drive top performers from your business.

Building a strong team that works together collaboratively can have an outsized impact on your business.

Performance Accelerator 1: Acquire the Right Skills and Capabilities, and Avoid Critical Mistakes

You've probably heard the saying, "Get the right people on the bus." It refers to getting top talent and all the skills you need to run your business. But getting on a bus and going for a ride is a passive activity. It suggests that once you are on the bus, going for a ride and not contributing is fine.

A different way of thinking about your team is as an orchestra. In an orchestra, everyone has a different sheet of music; they are all doing something different. But they are all outstanding players and need to work in complete harmony for the piece of music to be a success.

In your business, each of the chairs represents a different area. The most successful leaders know that for the business to outperform, no area of the business can be starved for talent.

Failure, Learning, and Fit: The Leadership Fundamentals

Years ago, I looked at hundreds, if not thousands, of business situations to see what made them successful or not, and why. It was the basis for developing an operational risk management system. I discovered that one of the largest risks was people.

People make the same mistakes through their careers. Some mistakes are around managing and leading people. Others are around how goals are set and monitored. And still others are around progressively larger business situations—managing the complexity of larger organizations and progress toward goals.

When people were put into situations wherein they had not yet made the mistakes and led at the scale of business, it proved problematic.

Stephen Babson at Endeavour Capital has a similar perspective. In looking at capabilities, he looks for people who have instinctive understandings of how businesses operate. It is a hard perspective to learn if you haven't been in a business and have only observed from it the outside.

In hiring people, these prove to be critical hiring points. Understanding the mistakes and learnings, as well as the ability to handle the scale and pace of the business, are critical in assessing fit. These are also key points in developing your people.

When considering who to hire, Wendy Collie not only listens to candidates' accomplishments, but asks candidates about their failures and what they learned along the way. The answers not only show what was learned and the acceptance of responsibility, but also highlight the character and belief systems of the individuals. In a high-performance organization, finding the right fit is important to the team and the organization.

In addition, Wendy also looks at whether individuals define their success through the success of others or through their own individual contribution (giving credit or taking credit). A value and interest in learning outside of one's function allows people to be collaborative as a team.

Hiring versus Developing Skills and Capabilities

The size of your business will influence how skills and capabilities are brought into the organization. If your business is growing quickly, you'll find the rate of business growth outpaces the growth of people's

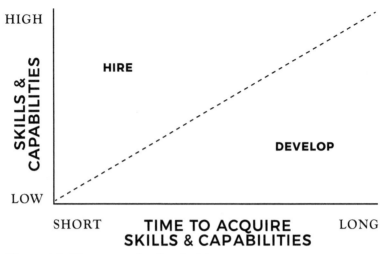

Figure 4.1 Hire versus develop decision map

capabilities. The need for higher skills (those that do not currently exist in your organization) combined with a short period of time means you need to hire. If you have a longer time period, the best course of action is to develop people internally.

Figure 4.1 gives a visual representation of when to hire versus when to build capabilities.

One of the most important but overlooked areas of business is the deliberate development of skills and capabilities of the people in that business. If you are in a large organization, you may be thinking that is not the case for you. And that may be true. But take a moment to pause and think about how many senior leaders are new to the organization versus internally developed.

There is a benefit to having outside perspectives, and we will cover that a bit later in this chapter. If that is the reason for the external hires, great! If the reason for hiring externally is there were no candidates qualified internally, then there is an opportunity to spend more time developing people.

To approach developing skills internally, for each position that exists today and is expected to exist in the next five years, outline the skills and capabilities needed to be successful.

Then, list each person that could be a candidate for that role. Next to their name, indicate if they are ready now for that position, or if they will be ready in five years—and what skills need to be developed to get there.

Projects or roles that will close the gaps should be identified. A deliberate conversation should be held with each person to discuss their interest in advancement, and the skills required to do so. At higher levels of the organization, relocation may be necessary, so having deliberate conversations is crucial. Those conversations may also uncover different desires.

As people grow within leadership roles, the need for more strategic perspectives grows. Their time is spent on more strategic activities. Conversely, people on the front lines tend to spend more time on tactical activities. Thus, every organization should have a balance of strategic and tactical capabilities.

Technical skills are more important early in one's career and on the front lines. As people grow and move into more senior roles, leadership skills become more important.

Balancing technical and leadership skills, as well as strategic and tactical mindsets, is necessary in every area of the business.

Communication and collaboration are the glue that holds the organization together.

Figure 4.2 presents visual way to think about this.

Depending on the size of your organization, this triangle can be very flat or very deep. As people progress up the ladder, they typically shed tactical and technical skills and focus on strategy and leadership. Being in a leadership role requires a new set of skills.

Each person has the capability to flex up and down through the triangle. For some, their capabilities band is narrow. For others, it is wide, meaning they can be both strategic and tactical as well as work on technical issues while leading people.

Figure 4.2 The talent triangle

As you build out your organization, think about how wide or narrow each band is. If you are in a small organization or a fast-growing organization, the bands of skills need to be wide—allowing for flexing without adding people. Conversely, in a large organization, the band may be narrow. When hiring people, understanding how wide the range of skill sets in your candidates is will determine how successful each individual and the company will be. Understanding this perspective will inform how you recruit or develop people.

What if you don't know what you need in your organization? The good news is there are a lot of paths to understanding how top organizations identify what talent is needed in the organization and how to attract it. Some of these are as follows:

- Surround yourself with people who have perspectives on what top-performing companies do. This includes advisers, bankers, and accountants.
- Get involved with trade organizations, and see what your top-performing competitors are doing.
- Follow thought leaders who discuss these topics—in magazines, books, podcasts, seminars, and so on.

Jim Hackett believes there is huge value in serving on other boards, so you can see how other companies operate, how other management teams think, and what trends may exist within and around your industry and in the greater population as a whole. Reading a great deal about your industry and what trends might exist and talking with other CEOs about what they see are also important. These perspectives will inform what skills you may need to infuse into your organization.

There are a variety of strategic and tactical reasons to seek skills and capabilities outside of your organization. You may decide that because of your size, you need certain skills and capabilities internally, while others you can contract with externally. Payroll, for example, is commonly outsourced. And strategic thinking may be obtained through board members or advisers.

Finding the right balance of what exists today and what is needed for the future—based on the strategy of the organization—should inform who is hired and when.

Performance Accelerator 2: Drive the Business with Top Talent—in the Right Place

You may be wondering why hiring top talent is included in a chapter about teams. Teams start with people. And bringing top people into your business, if done well, will spur your growth.

Top talent outperforms peers by as much as 10 times or more. But, what is top talent? How do you know it when you see it?

Expanding your exposure to different people, industries, perspectives, and business sizes will broaden your view on the level of talent in the marketplace. Advisers, business leaders, and thought leaders will round out your perspectives on what top talent is, focusing on various areas of business.

Heidi's High-Performer Indicators:

- Taking initiative
- Being accountable
- Leveraging others
- Communicating well
- Identifying and removing roadblocks
- Recognizing patterns
- Learning from failure
- Showing curiosity
- Demonstrating grit
- Holding strong values
- Displaying creativity
- Showing resourcefulness
- Proving coachable
- Focusing on results, not activity
- Not easily being distracted

You don't need top talent in every position. You just need it in key positions. Here's where you need it:

- C-suite
- Department heads

- Any position that requires strategic thinking
- Any position that requires innovation
- Any highly technical position that drives value

Regardless of top talent or not, the people you bring into the company should be excited about your company's purpose and have values that align with your organization's. The purpose and values set the foundation for the culture and operating norms. Your talent needs to be a good fit.

You are much better off bringing top talent into the business and paying them well rather than going on the cheap. Your compensation policies should be set to accommodate for this. While you may pay a little more for top talent, the results they generate will exceed, by far, the results of the average person.

Performance Accelerator 3: Find the Balance of People Who Have Been in the Organization and People New to the Organization

Throughout my career, I've had to evaluate teams and determine what skills were necessary in the areas of my responsibility as part of assuming leadership for departments, divisions, and businesses to deliver results. My role was typically to increase performance. Every single time, there have been people who were excited about making changes to elevate the organization and knew change was needed.

Even if you aren't new to the business and have been in place for some time, if you manage others, it is important to periodically step back and take stock of your team. The business will grow and change over time, and you may need to add new skills and capabilities.

People who have been in the business know:

- Their way around the business, systems, and processes
- What was tried in the past and why it worked or didn't
- The informal networks and influencers
- The pulse of the organization.

People who are coming from outside have:

- Perspectives about other business models that can be applied in your business
- An unbiased perspective about how well your business is performing
- Perspectives from customers and competitors that are keys to improving performance

If the team dynamics are working well, the people who are new to the organization should be pushing to try new things and make improvements. Those who have been there for some time will have perspectives about what will work and why, as well as the best approach to get there. The creative tension will get you better results.

Performance Accelerator 4: Create a Direct Line of Sight for Each Person to the Overarching Goals

In your business, getting the team galvanized around goals and working together seamlessly takes a bit more work. Goals and expectations need to be visible and discussed regularly. For every person on the team to understand where they fit into the goals, they need to see how they fit into the business. The best way to do this is to cascade the goals throughout the organization. Values are included in this process, as they drive how people behave in accomplishing goals. If you have a vision and/or a mission, they should be included here as well. Table 4.1 shows how goals can be cascaded for each person.

The beauty of going through this type of process (which should not be a long-drawn-out exercise) is that it removes competing goals. It puts each area of the business on the hook for accomplishing the goals of the organization and requires cross-functional discussion to make sure that resources are mobilized in the right way to accomplish the overall goals.

In operations or sales, it is easier to draw a straight line from the sales and operations goals for the year. But for many others in the business, it isn't as easy to draw a straight line. People want to know how they fit in and contribute to the goals.

I've used this model in a number of companies, because it shows people the direct line from the company goals to the individual goals. Each

Table 4.1 Cascading goals overview

Purpose	Why your business exists
Values	Value 1
	Value 2
	Value 3
	Value 4
	Value 5
Long-term Goals	Goal 1
	Goal 2
	Goal 3
Current-Year Company Goals	Goal 1
	Goal 2
	Goal 3
Department Goals	Goal 1
	Goal 2
	Goal 3
Individual Goals	Goal 1
	Goal 2
	Goal 3

department should be putting this together and sitting down as a team to share goals for the year. When you do this, you'll find your people are much more engaged and committed to advancing their goals.

In Chapter 6, we get into more detail about selecting and cascading information. There, you'll see the channels to discuss goals and progress on a regular basis.

Performance Accelerator 5: Bust through Resistance and Conflict

In general, people have good intentions and try to do what they believe is the right thing. Without clarity on roles and responsibilities, however, friction can grow. Here are some of the challenges that need to be worked through to have an effective team:

- People working in silos
- Unclear responsibilities
- Who makes decisions versus who provides input

As a leader, you set the tone in getting people together to work through issues and opportunities. Let's look at a few ways to resolve the aforementioned challenges.

Busting through Silos

The best way to bust through silos is to get people working together. Monthly business reviews and systems implementations are just a few activities that are cross-functional. The following is a specific example of how a cross-functional meeting can look:

- Successful organizations hold monthly meetings with a cross-functional team of sales, operations, and finance to review margin by customer and margin by product or service.
- Ideally, finance provides the reports that serve as the basis for discussion in a visual format. Even if you aren't in a senior leadership position, you can drive these meetings informally with your peers.
- Through the course of the conversation, operations should discuss any operating challenges or successes that impacted cost during the month and improvements being made to increase productivity.
- Sales should discuss pricing changes being made to increase profitability, competition in the market, and market dynamics. Finance can offer insight into the numbers and clear up any confusion there.

These types of conversations should happen across the organization on a regular basis.

The best way to ensure that teams work together in a cohesive manner is to involve people from departments that work together regularly to participate in hiring decisions. For example, hiring a financial analyst would involve the sales and operations team members that this person would be working with on a regular basis.

Clarifying Responsibilities

It seems like a simple thing to be clear about responsibilities, but many times there is a gap in expectations about those responsibilities, including working across functions. Written job descriptions and goals go a long way toward being clear about responsibilities.

Avoiding Misunderstandings around Decision Making

Decision making is an area of great consternation within teams. Tension usually arises from people believing they should have a say in a decision, and the other people believing they should not. So, how is this resolved?

The best way to agree on decision making is to agree to a process before being in the middle of making a critical decision. Here's what needs to be considered:

- Who has to approve?
- Who should be providing input?
- How is a tie broken if there is a 50–50 split when a vote is taken?
- Who has ultimate authority or final decision?

Some companies use a RACI (Responsible, Accountable, Consulted, and Informed) model to work through decision making. This model outlines who is responsible for making decisions, who has input (consulted for advice), and who is informed of decisions. It is usually completed in a great deal of detail so there is no confusion. And it is shared broadly so people know their role in the decision-making process.

Others have an authorization matrix that indicates who must approve high-level decisions such as capital projects and long-term agreements. The point is they think through all the decisions that are made and determine who will decide on everything from hiring to spending money to signing contracts.

Beyond making the decision is supporting the decision that was made. The worst thing that can happen within an organization is people in one area talking about how bad the decision was and undermining another part of the organization.

For each decision that was made, all of the right people were involved, discussions were held, and a decision was made. High-performing organizations have a clear decision-making process. When everyone walks out of the room, there should be a united front in supporting the direction and decision.

Performance Accelerator 6: Get Rid of Friction Points That Drive Top Performers from Your Business

One of the secrets of high-performing companies is that it is much easier to work in a top-performing company than one that is struggling to survive. Systems are designed to support work being done, processes are smooth, and decision making is fast and delegated to the right places in the business.

High-performing individuals perform best when the structure of the business and its systems and processes are designed to support getting things done, not hindering them. Here are a few questions to ask:

- How many approvals are necessary to get work approved?
- Do the systems require work arounds to get work done?
- Is it easy to get the necessary data to do the work?
- Is ownership of activities or areas clear?
- Is excessive time being spent in meetings or preparing reports?
- Does it take a long time to get anything done?
- Are people excited to show up every day?
- Do people talk about the systems being bureaucratic?

If the answers to any of these questions indicate it is hard to get work done, it is time to streamline. The reality is, you won't keep your best people if it is hard to work there.

Here's what this looks like in action. At Longview, there was no insight into the daily production operations when I arrived. Without it, there was no ability to see where the choke points were and what was slowing the operation down. An operating system was installed to monitor the speed of the equipment and the production levels.

Each day, the operators could pinpoint why a machine would go down or why a quality issue would crop up. There was no longer a need to guess. Mechanical problems that needed to be fixed would be addressed immediately, or in future scheduled maintenance, depending upon the urgency.

Meetings were eliminated across the organization, unless they were for making decisions. E-mail traffic was greatly diminished by dropping people off cc lines. And all the processes were overhauled to eliminate unnecessary steps.

Another way to help get rid of friction is to ensure the physical environment is conducive to getting work done. At Longview, one of the biggest performance boosters was an office remodel. Having an updated work environment with cubicle walls and ergonomically designed furniture that was comfortable and supported the work being done was a major boost to productivity and engagement.

In taking all of these actions, the company was able to increase output and profitability by orders of magnitude with a third less people.

Mitzi Perdue's father, Ernest Henderson (Sheraton's founder), was a big believer in this as well. Every time he would take over a new hotel, the first dollars he would spend were in areas the public would never see. He invested in employee dining rooms, showers, and elevators. He wanted the people to know they were the most important part of the operation: They would make the hotel a success or not. And when the people were given a better vision of themselves, they lived up to it and elevated the hotel's performance.

Your Team Actions

Business is all about people. No matter the industry, harnessing the power of the people is the key to success. In businesses that outperform, you'll typically find that the organization is performing well financially, people are having fun, and things are clicking. It's not an accident. Hard work and constant focus go into making the organization successful. Is your organization where you want it to be, from a team perspective? Here are a few questions to consider:

- What skills and capabilities do you need for today and the future that are not currently in your organization?
- What actions do you need in order to align goals throughout your organization?
- Where in your organization do you need top talent that does not exist today?
- What mechanisms do you need to implement to reduce resistance and conflict?
- What actions do you need to take to remove friction points?
- What other gaps do you need to close after reading this chapter, and what resources do you need to close them?

CHAPTER 5

Don't Settle for a Cult Following

The term *cult following* was originally coined to describe a small group of passionate people who were highly dedicated to a work of culture, such as a piece of art. Having a cult following is a great thing. Who wouldn't want passionate fans of their business? The point is, you can't have a large business with only a small group of passionate fans. That passion must translate to a larger customer base. And given the role of technology today, it is easier than ever to reach a broader audience.

Amazon has become a juggernaut in the business world by putting the customer at the center of everything they do. Its one-click shopping and Prime membership allow customers to quickly order and receive what they want. And many times, should an issue arise, it is quickly resolved to the satisfaction of the customer. Social media has provided customers with platforms to share their views, whether good or bad, about their customer and product experiences.

Amazon has talked about putting the customer at the center of their business so much it can sound cliché. But it is not. The customer drives everything!

Some businesses focus on competing with their competitors. They put a lot of energy there, and it is about winning.

Amazon takes a different approach: They get energy from the challenge of giving customers what they want. By putting the customer at the center of the business, Amazon must focus on innovation and not letting bureaucracy and process get in the way of serving the customer.

The customer-centric approach led Amazon to create its Prime program, a model that drives higher customer loyalty. According to chief executive Bezos, customers want low price, fast delivery, and a big selection. At one point, the company experimented with ad placements to get customers' attention and found that it did little for sales. Amazon was better off lowering cost and subsidizing shipping rather than running ads.

Amazon collects a significant amount of data on customers to recommend products they may like as well as to improve the buying experience. The information obtained has led the company to invest in a number of different areas—some that have been successful, and some that have not.

Bezos's belief in the long-term view of giving customers what they want and putting them at the center of the business results in a significant competitive advantage. Other companies are so focused on return on investment in the short term that they don't invest in platforms that can scale.

While the low-cost, fast-delivery model is a hallmark for the retail side of their house (online marketplace for individual consumers to buy goods), a very different approach is taken on the business side of the house (business services such as storing data and paying for data analytics). The core tenet of *customer at the center* is still in place.

Part of Amazon's business is its web services, Amazon Web Services (AWS). AWS makes a healthy profit and supports the retail side of the house. It does this by giving businesses what they need—flexibility in running their infrastructure and insights into their businesses.

AWS is the largest provider of cloud services to businesses in the world. Businesses no longer need to have server farms on their own sites to store data. AWS stores it for them in the cloud. Its customer-centric approach enables businesses to use the cloud for their hybrid needs.

With a hybrid infrastructure model, large corporations don't have to migrate their server infrastructure to the cloud and incur significant costs. The hybrid model allows them to keep their existing server infrastructure while adding storage capacity through the cloud.

The bulk of AWS's innovations (90 percent) is based on what customers ask for, with the balance coming from strategic *interpretations* of what customers ask for. These innovations include data analytics, machine learning, and mobile technology.

While Amazon earns a healthy margin on this side of the house, the total cost for the customer is often lower than with its competitors. Businesses are able to use existing infrastructure and seamlessly add on cloud capacity. This approach costs significantly less than scrapping an entire infrastructure and implementing another model from scratch, as the business only incurs the cost of the additional cloud capacity, not the cost of implementing an entirely new infrastructure.

It is no surprise that by tailoring their approach to customer needs, Amazon has consistently ranked number one in customer satisfaction by the American Customer Satisfaction Index for nine years through 2016. This same customer-centered approach has led to a nearly 35 percent market share of the cloud market worldwide in 2017, according Synergy Research. Amazon's customer-centric philosophy highlights three performance accelerators.

Pozzo Performance Accelerators:

1. Give customers what they value.
2. Put the customer first; don't let the process drive bad decisions.
3. Create situations where your people and your customers can be your evangelists.

The basis for making the customer-centric model work is *trust*. Amazon sticks to its approach of what is right for the customer, even if it hurts profitability in the short term. They have done this by replacing items that were delivered to an incorrect address or damaged in transit. Amazon figured out that by giving customers a great experience, they would share their experience with everyone they know. That in turn would fuel growth and build a strong, long-term business.

Performance Accelerator 1: Give Customers What They Value

People spend money on what they value. If your customer is strictly looking at what something costs, that is a commodity business and a tough place to be. Your goods or services are being viewed as indistinct to others, and you are playing a price game that typically goes in one direction: *down*.

Amazon tapped into what customers' value. For some, it is being able to compare products and make a decision without going to a bunch of stores. For others, it is the ability to quickly order online and get the product the next day, saving a bunch of time.

Longview made paper that was used in the manufacturing of bags. It was squarely in the commodity category with goods that could be manufactured by any number of companies around the world.

After getting to know the needs of a particular customer, it was apparent that the customer's machines were speed limited (could not run faster) on the basis of the three plies of paper being used. Longview realized it had access to raw materials that were not accessible to competitors, allowing it to produce a superior grade of paper. The superior paper would allow the customer to run its machines faster, and the customer would use only two plies instead of three—reducing its cost for the paper.

This innovation allowed the company to charge an increased price and the customer to have a lower cost; the process used less paper and produced more because the machines ran faster. Longview became known as a premium producer of the product, not just a commodity player. This innovation only came about after visiting the customer facility and asking the customer what they valued. It was a win–win.

New Seasons also gives customers what they want by ensuring each location reflect its' neighborhood in the design, product, and community involvement. Each of the stores curated their product mix to reflect their community. And each store is empowered to find ways to support their local customers. For example, one store had a staff member who knew sign language. There were a number of hearing impaired customers who had been struggling to shop. The signing staff member created a program to help them shop, as well as shared her work hours so they knew when they could find her. The hearing impaired customers valued this program.

There are a number of ways you can find what your customers value. Use this Customer Value Finder guide to discover what your customers value:

- Ask people at different levels in your customer's organization what is working well and what else you can be doing.
- Have a third party ask current and former customers—as well as companies that chose not to do business with you—what you are good at and for those that work with competitors, why they go with your competitors.
- Ask your people who work with customers in various parts of the organization what customers tell them.

- Ask your customers why their purchases are increasing or declining.
- Monitor your competitors' products or services, and see what is gaining traction.
- Ask your suppliers what they hear in the market.

Going through this process, you may find that there are products or services you don't sell but should. Maybe there are quality issues you need to address. Or maybe things are going really well, and you need to keep doing what you have been doing, because your customers are happy.

When customers are happy with the value you provide, it strengthens your brand and makes you top of mind when anyone wants to buy what you sell.

Performance Accelerator 2: Put the Customer First; Don't Let the Process Drive Bad Decisions

Nordstrom is legendary in the retail world for making sure the customer is pleased with each purchase. If something isn't working, Nordstrom takes it back. No hassles. Knowing people lose receipts, they attach a barcode to each tag that stores the information related to the purchase. They have designed the process to make it easy for customers to buy and return items. After all, customers return purchases. It is part of the retail industry. Making it as easy as possible builds customer loyalty.

Like Nordstrom, Amazon has made it easy for customers to buy products. After setting up a profile, a customer can purchase an item with one click. There is no multiple step process of validations, filling out information, and clicking through multiple screens to agree to the purchase.

Both Nordstrom and Amazon have made it easy to do business with them. They don't let bad processes get in the way of customers. And because of this, customers sing their praises.

Customer buying is a series of yeses. When "No" gets introduced into the mix, it frustrates customers and drives them to buy elsewhere.

Here are a few warning signs indicating that you may need to change some processes to put your customers first. Your people regularly say:

- "*There's nothing we can do about that*" (in response to a customer issue).

- *"We need you to fill out these forms before we can proceed."*
- *"The person who needs to approve the transaction isn't here."*
- *"We don't have it at this location, but it is available at the other location across town."*
- *"We are out of stock of this item; it will be a few weeks before it is back in stock."*

Businesses that have cult followings have learned that roadblocks to doing business need to be eliminated. In businesses that outperform, the aforementioned situations don't happen. Instead, this is what you expect to see:

- *"Here's what we can do to resolve that issue. Does that work for you?"* (This requires giving frontline people authority for making decisions to resolve issues for customers—and training on how to do this.)
- *"We've loaded your history into our system from your prior transactions. If it looks OK, we are ready to proceed."*
- *"We are ready to proceed without any further approvals."*
- *"We have this item in our location across town. I'd be happy to ship it to you overnight at no additional cost."*
- Stock-out situations rarely occur; purchasing data is transmitted to suppliers, so restocking happens before it is a problem.

The key to making a seamless customer experience is to understand where the choke points are in your business and your competitors' businesses. By eliminating them, you put the focus on your product or service, not on the process of getting it.

Cult followings come from customers getting what they value and having great experiences.

Performance Accelerator 3: Create Situations Where Your People and Your Customers Can Be Your Evangelists

People buy products or services based on recommendations from others they trust. Word of mouth is the most effective form of advertising by far—more than any other medium. How then do you leverage the praises of your customers into evangelist marketing?

Think back to the last time you spoke with someone who just ordered something from Amazon. They probably shared that they needed to get a certain type of product. They went onto Amazon and found a few options, read through the reviews, clicked a button, and the next day had that product in their hands. It was fantastic! So the next time you needed to buy something, instead of jumping into the car and heading down to the store, you bought the desired item through Amazon.

It wasn't through advertising that Amazon made its greatest gains; it was through word of mouth. So how do you bring that into your business? You need to create evangelists in your customer base. Here's how:

The Evangelist Generator

- Create communities for people to connect.
- Bring your customers and prospective customers together.
- It is easier to move customers up from one level to the next.

Mitzi Perdue shared stories about how she and her late husband, Frank, supported their people at Perdue Chicken. There was a flood in North Carolina that wiped out the homes and livelihoods of 70 of their associates. Frank sent checks for $1,000 out of his own pocket (not the company's) to each of the people, plus $100 in cash. He knew that the people would need money to buy groceries to get through the weekend and arranged for the checks and cash to be delivered to each family.

Mitzi and Frank viewed the employees as part of the family. They visited people in the hospital or when they were retired and went to weddings and funerals. They engendered a loyalty and appreciation from their associates. Because they were valued, their associates became evangelists for the company.

Create Communities for People to Connect

You probably belong to at least one, maybe more, communities for users of a product or service. It may be a club, such as a fitness club or wine club. Or, it could be an online community for discussing new products or troubleshooting issues for something like Apple's products.

The communities engage members about their likes, dislikes, and new offerings. The members do a lot of the work in spreading messages and sharing tips with each other. More than that, this creates a level of engagement, belonging, and loyalty.

Starting a community takes a bit of work. The forum needs to be created, and access should be relatively easy. To encourage people to participate initially, new offerings should be shared there first, and all communications should be funneled there to drive traffic.

The Multnomah Athletic Club (MAC) in Portland, Oregon, has mastered the art of creating a community. Founded in 1891, the MAC is ranked number two by the Platinum Clubs of America. The club includes world-class athletic facilities and social offerings, including fine dining and meeting space. Generations of families are amongst the membership base of roughly 20,000 people.

The MAC creates community by involving people in the operations of the club. Each year, hundreds of people are involved in the club's committee system, giving input on the offerings in each area of the club. This approach serves to connect members to the club and to each other.

The community is so strong that the MAC has capped its membership to ensure the member experience is always highly positive. Every three or so years, a lottery process is held to identify and prioritize new members who will be admitted as openings arise. Those joining the club have heard about and visited the club and are excited to join.

New Seasons has also been successful at creating communities with its customers. Because it is a community and neighborhood store, people connect there with friends and neighbors. Senior day on Wednesday has become a ritual for many people. The day begins with coffee, sharing stories about kids and grandkids, and laughing about everything. Coffee is followed by shopping, then by lunch, and more shopping. The store is designed to facilitate these connections.

Bring Your Customers and Prospective Customers Together

There is nothing better than having your customers tout your products or services to other customers. It is one thing for you to share how great you think your product is. Having your customers sing your praises to potential customers is a much more effective approach. A customer appreciation event where you invite current customers and top prospective customers is one way you can get customers sharing their experiences.

Alan Weiss has mastered bringing customers and prospective customers together. Alan has a vibrant consulting community that is very active. On a daily basis, people interact on a closed online forum by asking questions and sharing insights.

Throughout the year, Alan offers programs that range from small, intimate, focused gatherings (usually with top customers) to large gatherings that include both people who are longtime customers and those who are there for the first time.

The content of the meetings is high. It is targeted at the group of people attending and includes time for socializing. During this time, people speak to each other and find shared values and interests.

When varied groups of customers and potential customers are brought together, current customers can share the value they are receiving. When customers are happy, such as in Alan's community, they do the selling for you.

Here are a few ways to do this:

- Host a customer appreciation event to thank your customers for their business.
- Host a technical conference to connect operations people with your customers to allow for an exchange of ideas.
- Hold a market and products session to discuss what is going on with your markets and the upcoming products that will address changing needs.
- Hold an investor fair for investors to tour your facility and hear about the latest trends in your business.
- Hold an informal holiday party to bring customers and potential customers together.

The Portland Art Museum (PAM) is focused on not being just a place where people come to view objects. It is about creating experiences for people—and that experience will be different for everyone, creating a rich and exciting cultural experience.

In the fall of 2017, PAM collaborated with Oregon beer brewers to create an event in conjunction with the museum's 125th anniversary. The exhibit, Picturing Oregon, pulled images from six distinct geographic areas in Oregon. Brewers from different parts of the state created special, high-quality beer that was reflective of or inspired by the pictures. A full-day event drew in nearly 500 people to hear the brewers talk about their techniques in the morning with tours of the exhibits and beer tasting in the afternoon.

PAM's ongoing creative approaches to connecting the community in different ways to the museum brings longtime members and people new to the museum bonding over shared passions.

The right approach for you will depend on the size of your business and the geographic footprint of your customers.

It Is Easier to Move Customers Up from One Level to the Next

Your current customers already know and love you. They know your offerings and what to expect from you. It is much easier to convert them to a higher level of engagement and sales than to convert a prospective customer to a customer.

It is important to understand whether your customers have more capacity to buy from you. This can occur if they are growing, you believe you can accelerate their earnings, or they are buying from you as well as your competitors. If you are providing high value to your customers and they have more capacity to buy, you will both be better off by working more closely together.

By getting top customers talking to your next best customers, you can encourage a stronger relationship. An example is for your top customers to share how in working together, new solutions were generated that propelled their business to the next level.

You are creating a gravitational pull with your business. The stronger the value perceived, the faster customers will move closer to your business. This movement is reflected in Figure 5.1.

A construction company I worked with was able to make this jump successfully. One of its clients was building basically the same facility in several locations across the country. Each location had a few design

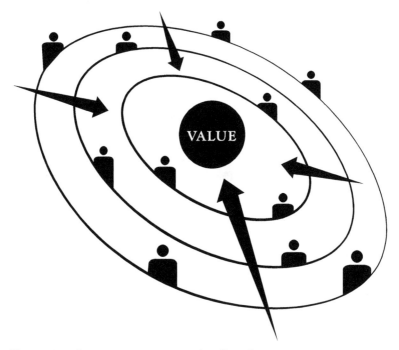

Figure 5.1 Creating a gravitational pull with your customers

specifications that were unique to the location. However, each design was basically the same. So, the construction company was contracted for most of the locations.

By creating a relationship between themselves and building trust, both parties were better off. The construction company was able to adjust the design for each location more easily. The execution plan to build was relatively similar between locations. The company also could source the materials in a manner that was cost effective. And because the relationship was known, each step was streamlined.

Because of the synergies, the customer's cost went down, and they were able to get their facilities up and running more quickly—generating an earlier online revenue stream. The construction company had a guaranteed stream of work without the time and expense of bidding for each of the facilities individually.

Both parties were happy and better off. In this case, moving up to the next level meant that there wasn't an individual series of projects that was bid on—some won and some lost. Rather, they had an ongoing agreement for all construction of this type of facility.

Your Actions

Having a broad group of fans that includes customers, employees, suppliers, and other stakeholders can do more for you than any advertising campaign. A large fan base of customers tells that market that you are *the* business in your market. People will want to buy your products or services, work for you, or invest in your business. This can only happen if people are singing your praises. Consider the following:

- How can you provide your customers with what they value in a way you aren't currently doing?
- What processes or experiences do you need to address to improve your customers' buying experience?
- What steps do you need to take to create or strengthen a community with your customers?
- What events are you scheduling to bring your customers together?
- What other gaps do you need to close after reading this chapter, and what resources do you need to close them?

PART III

Keeping Score and Reaching New Heights

CHAPTER 6

You Can't Outperform
If You Don't Keep Score

Imagine driving into a paper mill site. The entire facility is green from World War II army-surplus paint, moss covers most of the roofs, and many people in the community believe the business has a high probability of not surviving.

The owners, however, believed the business could survive with a lot of work.

That was the situation at Longview when I arrived.

The few of us brought in by the new owners knew that a rapid transformation was necessary. And we knew that transparency and accountability relative to targets were necessary to make rapid progress.

Having a comprehensive approach to measuring progress, holding people accountable, and keeping score were fundamental to the rapid progress. When I joined the company, however, none of what I outline in this chapter was in place. Only a few people had seen the financial results: The business had not performed well financially, and the people responsible for running each area of the business were not aware of it.

At the beginning of the transformation, each leader of the various areas of the business was given clear accountability for achieving results. At the same time, working collaboratively across functions and locations was important to achieving success.

Early on, we convened monthly business reviews with key managers and weekly meetings with senior leaders to review progress against goals. In the early days, closing the gaps wasn't easily pinpointed and articulated. Eventually, as key resources were added, the path to closing gaps was identified and rapidly addressed.

As the level of understanding and engagement evolved, trends in the business were evaluated. Whether products, environment, customers, or regulatory issues, changes were incorporated into how business was conducted. All employees knew what was going on and how to focus.

Each leader was responsible for his or her area of the business. Goals were established, and progress against them was measured daily, weekly, or monthly—depending upon the area. Charts and graphs highlighted progress and trends. The visual depiction of results, along with key performance indicators (KPIs), drove fact-based conversations and a focus on key points.

To drive transparency throughout the organization, guests from around the organization were included in quarterly business review meetings. Town hall meetings were held across all locations to cover everything from financial results to progress against goals. It was important for people at all levels to understand the goals and see how business was conducted.

The approach to setting targets and keeping score was fundamental to making rapid progress against financial and performance targets. In less than five years, and through the economic downturn in 2008, the organization nearly tripled EBITDA. This approach highlights four performance accelerators.

Pozzo Performance Accelerators:

1. Define success, related targets, and KPIs.
2. Report against targets regularly.
3. Hold people accountable for achieving results.
4. Create multiple channels to share targets and progress across the organization.

Setting targets and keeping score sound easy when you read about them. But to make these work in practice requires people at all levels engaging and owning their part. We'll dive into each concept in depth to give you the tools that top-performing businesses use. But before we do, complete the assessment in Table 6.1 to see how you stack up right now.

Table 6.1 The outperforming scoreboard assessment

	Yes	No
Do you have clear goals for the year?		
Are they measurable?		
Do you have KPIs (topic explained later in this chapter) that accurately capture progress against those goals?		
Are your KPIs tracked:		
In real-time?		
Daily?		
Weekly?		
Monthly?		
Are people held accountable for accomplishing their goals?		
Do you have incentive plans that align pay with performance?		
Do you have monthly business reviews?		
Are you communicating progress to the entire organization no less than quarterly?		

How are you doing in measuring and sharing your results?

- If you had 10 to 11 questions marked "Yes," congratulations! You are performing well. But don't stop reading. There are a number of tips that will help you get even better.
- If you had eight to nine questions marked "Yes," you are doing well and just need to shore up a few areas. You'll find actionable steps you can take now to focus your organization on performance.
- If you had seven or fewer questions marked "Yes," you have lots of opportunity to increase performance in your organization. With some effort, this is one of the easiest areas to gain traction quickly and will have the biggest impact on your organization. Let's get started!

Performance Accelerator 1: Define Success, Related Targets, and KPIs

For many, success is defined in terms of dollars. But dollars are an outcome of everything you do in business. It is a trailing indicator. For example, to increase sales, a lot of groundwork needs to be laid before sales start coming in. Conversely, taking focus off what customers value, whether the product or how you interact with your customer, will eventually result in lower sales. Thus, measuring success needs to be a combination of progress against the inputs necessary to achieve what you want and the financial outcome measures.

Stephen Babson looks at success as progress against goals—the climbing of rungs of a ladder. Financial success is a function of this progression. Tom Hellie's view is similar: He defines success as being able to rally everyone to fulfilling the vision.

Brian Ferriso views success at the art museum through the lens of three pillars:

- Acquire great and diverse works of art.
- Make art accessible—both physically and explaining it in a way that non-scholars can understand.
- Be fiscally responsible and transparent.

These perspectives all have one thing in common: There is no finish line. Success is a journey.

When I joined Longview as a senior leader, we set financial, production, and productivity goals. We shared them widely, along with what it would take to achieve those goals. But the real measure of success was creating a long-term, stable business. If the business performed well, it would support the community and retain jobs for the people that worked there.

Wherever you are in your journey, it is important to define what success is in the short term and what it is in the long term. The following are a few general goals you may consider:

- Grow sales
- Improve productivity
- Gain market share
- Introduce a new product or service
- Improve customer satisfaction

By clearly outlining what you are trying to accomplish and why, the entire organization can participate. As goals are set, they should be connected all the way through the organization. Recall, we walked through an example of how to do this in Chapter 4.

As an example, in a manufacturing environment, connecting goals through the organization means that the number of goods produced is broken down by day and shared with production people, the pricing by product and the number of products to be sold are shared with salespeople, and the cost structure is broken down by person and by department.

Increased productivity is fleshed out such that any capital expenditures or initiatives that are being implemented have both costs and production gains included in the targets. People clearly understand what improvements are being made, how it will impact them, and what the expected increase in output is.

Key Performance Indicators (KPIs)

KPIs, if designed well, allow people at every level of the business to self-monitor performance. They are the building blocks of the actions being taken in the organization that drive financial results. Ultimately, the actions taken and the results achieved inform the goals, becoming a feedback loop as depicted in Figure 6.1.

KPIs seem very obvious and discussed by everyone. The challenge is, many businesses don't select the right KPIs and/or have too many of them. The key is to choose the right ones that inform how the business is operating.

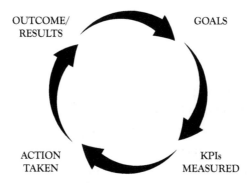

Figure 6.1 The performance feedback loop

Fundamentally, operating results can be viewed as follows:

$$\text{Volume} \times \text{Margin}$$

Measuring volume is easy. It is the number of hours worked and billed in a services business, or saleable goods produced and sold in a manufacturing firm. In a university environment, volume could be the number of students enrolled. In a museum, volume could be the number of visitors and members.

Harder to measure is the margin, which is revenue less cost. Revenue is easy, cost can get convoluted. Many times, allocations and accounting gyrations find their way into the cost, disconnecting it from reality and making the margin less predictable.

Each business will have its own KPIs based on the industry. But there are fundamental indicators that run across any business in any industry. When thinking about KPIs, they should be tracked internally and benchmarked to other companies in your industry. Here's what you should be looking at in your business.

Impact and Sustainability Measures

Impact and sustainability measures reflect the health of the organization. They include safety performance, waste, water usage, energy usage, and environmental impact, to name a few. These measures offer insight into your business. Businesses that outperform have strong impact and sustainability results as well as strong financial records. And that is not a mistake. Businesses that care about their people and impact on the community do a better job at managing every aspect of their business.

Cash Conversion Cycle

The cash conversion cycle is one of the most important metrics out there. It outlines in days how long it takes to build inventory, pay suppliers, and get paid by customers. It is a comprehensive measure and can be incredibly illuminating if you haven't looked at your working capital this way before. When you compare with others in your industry, you can quickly see whether you are using more cash to fund your business than others. Businesses that outperform manage cash intensely and minimize its use in the business.

EBITDA and EBITDA Margin

There can be a lot of noise in trying to benchmark financial results. A number of differences exist in how companies structure their operations that impact the comparison of interest, tax, and depreciation. These differences arise from how assets are financed and from debt levels, to name a few. EBITDA (earnings before interest, tax, depreciation, and amortization) removes those differences and gets to the operations of the company. EBITDA also removes the noncash charges that can distort the picture of how well the business is performing.

EBITDA margin (EBITDA divided by revenue) eliminates size as a factor in comparing businesses in the same industry and across industries. This allows you to get a good starting point as to how your profitability stacks up against others. From there, you can start peeling back each component to narrow in on where you are doing well, or where you can improve.

Volume Measures

Depending upon your industry, the measures that are tracked to show progress will vary. If your industry is manufacturing, the daily measure would be quantity of products produced. In construction, it would be how much is built in the day by area. In a retail business, it would be how much is sold by category.

Productivity should also be measured, indicating how much is produced in a given time frame. It may be how quickly a machine runs or how much work is accomplished in an hour. Whatever the measures in your industry, you should be tracking how much is produced in a specified period of time. The goal is to maximize the amount produced or sold in the given time. Businesses that outperform produce more per hour than their peers.

Indicators for Growth or Decline

Depending upon the business you are in, there are economic indicators that impact whether your business will be cycling up or down. The indicator may be housing starts or the price of oil or consumer spending. Whatever the indicator is, you should be tracking it and speaking with customers about it. Understanding what causes your customers to start or stop buying will allow you to adjust the direction of your business and not get caught short.

Customer Satisfaction and Buying Habits

You don't have a business if you don't have customers. Understanding how satisfied your customers are with you will signal if your business will increase or decline. Are others happy with your products or services? Are they only buying from you because there is no other option? Are they sharing their preferences and challenges? Your customers will have insights into what you need to do next.

In addition to understanding the satisfaction of your customers, it is important to understand their *spend* and if it is with you. Looking at your share of their spend, whether purchases are increasing or decreasing, and the frequency of their purchases, will inform you as to any opportunities or challenges. These are seen in retention and attrition rates. Spend is tracked and reported by a variety of organizations depending upon what you sell. If you sell a commodity item, many times the U.S. government tracks it. Industry associations also track and report spend. In addition, your banker or auditor may have this information.

One watch-out in designing KPIs is understanding if they are being gamed by the people in the organization. Here are a few ways this happens:

- Increasing production to meet daily goals, but quality declines, requiring rework.
- Not starting the clock until the completion time is within desired limits. Examples of this are folks at the drive-through not taking your order until the kitchen can make it in time, or a doctor's office not checking you in until the doctor is ready to see you.
- Moving budgets around to avoid showing an overrun.

The purpose of KPIs is to show whether progress is being made against goals—and have robust discussions if things are not on track.

Understanding the difference between data and information is integral to this process. Data is a bunch of numbers that may or may not have any meaning. It doesn't necessarily lead people to the right conclusions.

The key to getting your KPIs right is identifying the levers that if pulled have an impact on your business—and presenting them in a way that leads people to understand if things are on track or if levers need to be pulled. For some, this is second nature. For others, it may be tough to find. Sometimes it takes outside help to get to the real drivers of your business.

Performance Accelerator 2: Report against Targets Regularly

It is not enough to publish what you plan to do for the year as a business and then leave it alone—or just share it with management and keep it a secret to others. People at all levels need to see progress against goals on a regular basis. For those on the front line, that means every day.

At Longview, we looked at a variety of KPIs daily, weekly, and monthly. In a manufacturing business, if you start getting behind early in the month, waiting until the end of the month to evaluate production is too late. You never catch up. So, having KPIs set in a way that allows for managing the business is critical to outperforming.

It is important to note that in addition to reporting against KPIs, major initiatives are also discussed. These are the basis for growth and efficiencies. If done thoughtfully, they have a significant return on the investment made.

Reporting should be automated and delivered to appropriate people through a variety of means. Most people won't go into a system and pull results from the prior day, so pushed out reporting is important. Daily reports should be posted to bulletin boards, displayed on monitors, and discussed in daily meetings. It is important to get the information to people that they need to know to be most effective in their jobs. That information will vary based on position in the organization.

Depending on the level of technology investments, some reports may be e-mailed. In other cases, the information may be available in dashboards customized for each person to show relevant metrics and progress against them. Following are categories of reports and how they are used.

See Appendix B for a comprehensive compendium of reports you would expect to see in a manufacturing environment. While you may be in a different industry, it will give you a perspective to work from in filling in gaps you may have in your reporting structure.

Real-Time Reports

These reports are typically associated with operations and let frontline people know if they are producing at the pace necessary to achieve the expected results for the day. They would include production rates and throughput. People can act to adjust performance accordingly.

Daily Reports

These reports should be pushed out daily and made available in a manner that is appropriate for the people who need to see them. In some cases, e-mail may not be available, so posting in a visible place or showing results on a display would be appropriate. These reports would include sales, production, cash, and so on. Many companies have daily operations meetings to discuss issues and progress. These meetings are a good place to discuss progress.

Weekly Reports

These reports are in addition to the daily reports—which are focused on the building blocks to get to financial targets. The weekly reports are typically focused on working capital to ensure that working capital (accounts receivable, unbilled work, and inventory) is not building. Weekly reports also allow for progress against initiative or projects. These reports, coupled with the daily reports, would be included in an executive dashboard that gives a high-level perspective about whether the business is on track to achieve goals. These details should be discussed in weekly senior management meetings.

Monthly Reports

These reports bring together the pieces being reviewed daily. They take a higher-level perspective—which is the basis for making course corrections in the business—as they show cross-functional views of results. These reports include financial results, margin by customer, capital expenditures, banking compliance, and so on. Ideally, these reports would be reviewed by cross-functional teams to see what is going well and what needs to be done by whom to improve results.

Performance Accelerator 3: Hold People Accountable for Achieving Results

The biggest differentiator in achieving results (or not) is in having people understand their part in achieving the results, believe they are achievable, and own the targets that relate to them. This requires involving people in the target development and not just forcing numbers on them. There are a few times when issuing targets makes sense—typically in a turnaround situation.

People usually have good ideas about how to continue growing and improving, so their input into the process is crucial. Mulally found this to be the case when solving challenges at Ford. The answers didn't reside in the executive suite: They were found on the floor with the folks who did the work every day.

A balance between vision and direction set by leadership and tactics and ideas found by the folks across the organization is necessary to achieve results. Once they buy into where the company is going and the target results, people will own their part.

Here are a few ways that ownership and accountability for results can be achieved:

- Managers submit their budgets for the year and report against them on a monthly basis.
- Individuals determine their own goals for the year in concert with the overall organizational goals.
- Individuals discuss how they are doing against goals in front of peers in project meetings, daily production meetings, or departmental meetings.

People want to be on a winning team and be appreciated for their contributions. Incentive plans are a great way to get everyone focused on achieving the goals of the organization. Simple is always best. A short-term incentive plan may be based on the company achieving a certain level of earnings and one other key metric that significantly impacts the business. Then each person has specific goals that support the overall company direction, which can be used to adjust their incentive payment based on individual performance.

This was a very successful approach at Longview. People knew the goals and worked toward them. They were set in a way that fostered rapid progress with ambitious, but reasonable, goals that paid people for achieving results.

Jim Hackett used this approach at Anadarko as well. Incentives were paid to all employees on the basis of safety, cash flow, stock price, reserves, and production. To keep people engaged, progress was discussed regularly and posted in the elevator banks.

In addition to providing financial incentives, recognize people publicly for milestone achievements—not just longevity, but performance achievements. This can be done through the quarterly town hall meetings, or quarterly or annual dinners with family members present to recognize achievement.

From an external perspective, apply for awards in areas where the company is active. They can be for charitable acts performed by employees, through industry organizations for outstanding performance or innovation, or through state or local business organizations for achievement across a variety of categories. Receiving an external award can be exciting and empowering for the team—especially if people from all levels of the organization accept the award.

Performance Accelerator 4: Create Multiple Channels to Share Targets and Progress across the Organization

People can achieve targets only if they know what the targets are and how they play a part in achieving them. And this can only happen if everyone in the organization knows his or her part.

For example, if you are increasing sales by 10 percent for the year, what are the goals for each salesperson that adds up to at least 10 percent? What does that mean for production or service? Is more capacity needed through additional people or equipment? You get the idea. By cascading through a goal-setting process, all people in the business know their part and how they support the larger goal of growing sales by 10 percent.

Targets should be specifically broken down and discussed widely across the organization, in departments, and as part of individual performance discussions, as discussed in Chapter 4.

Many times, it is easy to miss the "back office" in the discussions, but it has an important role too. Whether it is getting information out more quickly to make decisions, supporting incremental hiring, or implementing new systems to support growth, each part of the organization needs to lock targets together to ensure there are no conflicts in achieving goals.

Quarterly town hall meetings are a great way of keeping people connected to what is going on in the business, changes in customer or product/service offerings, trends in the industry or with competitors, and so on. This is also a key time to share progress against goals of the organization. The quarterly town halls need to be substantive and include the opportunity for dialogue about any of the issues of the day.

Jim Hackett used this approach when he invited groups of 12 at a time in his first CEO job at Seagull Energy to an hour-long session to share the strategy and tactics of the business, and the values of the business and what they meant to him. People's current concerns or questions were also covered. He did this in a larger company, Anadarko, through monthly luncheons and town hall meetings.

Key topics in quarterly town hall meetings should include the following:

- Financial results/progress against goals
- Sales opportunities and customer feedback/preferences
- Product or service innovations or enhancements (or fixes to problems that have occurred)
- The overall economic environment and how it is impacting the industry
- A perspective on what is going on with competitors
- Recognition of key milestones or accomplishments
- Time for Q&A

The meetings should involve a number of people across sales, operations, and finance in key management roles, as well as senior leaders. This shows alignment in focus, as well as gives people the opportunity to hear from the folks who are making things happen in the organization. However it is done, the information should be consistent across all locations, with additional site-specific information as appropriate.

Between town hall meetings, there are a number of methods to share progress against achieving targets with the broader organization:

- Leaders at multiple levels should walk around, visit sites, and speak with people about the organization and its objectives—and listen to what is going well and where challenges exist.
- Daily and weekly meetings should occur with department managers and project leads to discuss progress against targets.
- Companywide newsletters can highlight key projects, wins, new products, and successes.

The point is, if you think you have communicated a lot, you probably haven't quite communicated enough. Information is asymmetric. You already know it, because you hear about it every day and have thought a lot about what needs to get done. Your people may have only heard about expectations and aspirations a few times. That's a big gap. I've found it takes half a dozen to a dozen repetitions in both writing and verbally for the message to be received.

Frank Perdue, Mitzi Perdue's late husband, also knew communication was essential. Mitzi shared stories about how she and Frank invited all of the Perdue Chicken employees to their house for dinner. Three times a month for 17 years, dinners were held with groups of employees 100 at a time. People came dressed casually, and they played various games such as horse shoes, badminton, tennis, or volleyball before dinner. While the goal was to entertain all 20,000 associates, they didn't quite get to entertaining everyone.

Frank shared the most current information about the company: what was going well and what wasn't. He continually communicated and reinforced messages. As a result, people felt connected to the company.

Figure 6.2 shows an approach to thinking about how often to communicate and with whom. For example, in the monthly business reviews, the C-Suite and key leaders discuss full company results. Key leaders and

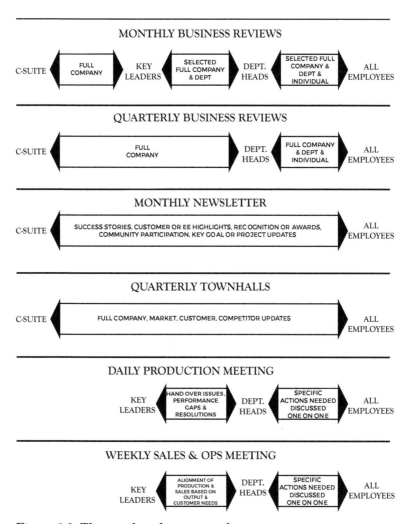

Figure 6.2 The scoreboard connector diagram

department heads discuss selected full company and department results. Department heads and all employees discuss selected full company, department, and individual results.

Your Actions

High-performing leaders know how their company stacks up internally, as well as against others in the industry. They use that information to gain competitive advantage. Finding the right combination of metrics is key to judging how well your company is doing. At a high level, there are typically only a few metrics that will matter, and they are not all financial. What do you need to do to close gaps in your organization? Consider the following:

- What is success to you? What actions do you need to take to share your view with your organization?
- Are your KPIs representative of your business or department? What actions do you need to take to refine them and share them more broadly within your organization?
- What mechanisms do you need to put into place to ensure progress against targets is being tracked?
- Are goals shared widely and people held accountable for achieving them? If not, what actions do you need to take to increase accountability?
- Are you regularly sharing progress with your organization or department? What else can you do to increase visibility?
- What other gaps do you need to close after reading this chapter, and what resources do you need to close them?

CHAPTER 7

If You Are Setting a Bar, It Is Already Too Low

When I was hired to be the CFO at Longview Fibre, the company had just been purchased by a private-equity firm. It was the end of 2007, and the need to make progress was readily apparent, given the low level of earnings based on the revenue stream. The people who had worked there for years knew things needed to change, but not how much.

We rolled out a financial target to more than double EBITDA. But most of the people—even those in the management ranks—had never seen the financial results of the business. We initiated a catchphrase to go along with the target to make it easy to remember, and we discussed the goal frequently across the organization.

As a leadership team, we knew there was a path to success. But for the organization, it seemed like an insurmountable hill ahead.

So, how do you close the gap between what you believe is a reasonable goal and what your people believe is a hill too high?

It starts with transparency and showing people what is possible.

In the case of Longview, we looked at where we were making or losing money—and revealed the untapped potential for equipment to help us.

We were quickly able to identify a number of products that were losing money and did not make sense to produce. Other companies produced them much better than we did. We also found several areas where we were undercharging customers for products based on market conditions.

On the equipment side, paper machine productivity by type of paper produced is measured in the United States and across the world by a third party. Machines are ranked based on the type of paper they make, so businesses can tell where their machines stack up. We were at the bottom of the productivity ranks in every type of paper produced.

Addressing these opportunities was sometimes as easy as asking some-one to run a machine faster. Other times, it took capital expenditures or addressing issues during maintenance outages.

With these opportunities identified, closing the gap to double EBITDA was definitely achievable. Getting people on board with the vision involved getting key influencers and managers to see the path and buy into the future.

As the buy in gained momentum across the organization, the hill did not seem so insurmountable. Then it became within reach.

Along the way, the recession hit the company in 2008—requiring swift action to adjust the product mix to keep the business full enough and gain operational capabilities.

We blew by that initial goal in just over 2 years, even with the reces-sion. As it turned out, when we looked across the business as a whole, there were opportunities everywhere. No area of the business was immune. By looking everywhere, the pace of the organization was in lockstep and it was operating as a high-performing business.

People will live up to the expectations you set, as long as they are achievable and there is a path. And far too often, that bar is actually too low, even if you think it is high. There are four lessons we can take away from the transformation at Longview.

Pozzo Performance Accelerators:

1. Goals should be ambitious, known to everyone, and the center of focus.
2. People need to see the path to get there.
3. People need to understand the market and competition.
4. Celebrate success and remind people of progress.

Stephen Babson looks for shrewdness in this area. The distinction in high-performing leaders is they know how to actually make things hap-pen. They know what resources are needed, what the key decisions are, and how to order them.

Achieving ambitious goals doesn't just happen. They require a focused effort of helping people see the path. It is equally important not to set the goal too low, as most of the time, people will stop and declare victory once they reach the finish line.

Performance Accelerator 1: Goals Should Be Ambitious, Known to Everyone, and the Center of Focus

The goals at Longview seemed more than ambitious at first. They seemed impossible to most people. But what we were really looking at was moving from the bottom of the pack to the middle, then from the middle toward the top.

Seems realistic, right? Once people understood that, the goals seemed much more attainable. Once the *what* was laid out, then it became about *when.*

The timeframe to make the leap seemed much more ambitious. We did set out to do a lot in a short timeframe.

The trick to attaining goals is they need to be realistic and push people to achieve their full potential in a way that collectively moves the organization forward. Setting ambitious goals requires a solid understanding of the capabilities of the organization—people, equipment, capital, and so on—as well as competitors and the general market.

So, how do you make a lot of progress quickly, especially when people aren't used to moving at that speed? For us, there was a combination of key hires who had made improvements quickly and outside resources dedicated to specific improvements.

Sometimes it takes bringing in people from outside of the industry or from high-performing competitors to understand the true capabilities of the organization.

Figure 7.1 depicts how to prioritize your actions on the basis of return and resources available.

Our rule of thumb was every project had to have a payback of less than 1 year. That caused us to think about appropriate scopes and ensuring the results were captured right away.

In the case of Longview, the business lagged behind competitors rather significantly. But what if you aren't lagging behind that much? The first thing is not to get complacent. If you do, you will find you fall behind quickly.

The world is changing quickly today. What used to take 10 years to accomplish can be done in two to three today. With that in mind, the bar

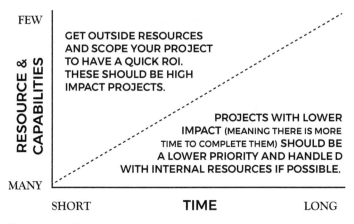

Figure 7.1 Prioritization and resourcing matrix

should be set with a two- to three-year time horizon. Move quickly to accomplish those goals, and continue to reset along the way.

Here are a few things you should consider in setting your bar:

- *The economy cycles* every 5 to 7 years, usually with 5 years in expansion and 1 year in contraction. Businesses that outperform gain ground as the economy starts cycling down and when it starts picking up. The reason is they have early warning indicators that tell when the economy is shifting. Based on that, they can outperform peers and gain ground. In setting your bar, economic cycles should be considered.

- In Chapter 3, we looked at *the pace of innovation.* You can set your bar properly only if you know what your customers value. You'll have some misses in there, but you won't be able to achieve your goals if what you are doing is not in line with what customers are buying. So, having strong relationships with your customers and understanding their buying habits is even more critical today.

- *Technology is rapidly changing the way business is done.* Depending on your industry, the impact of technology will vary. To stay in front of technological changes requires close alignment with your suppliers, along with what is in development right now. Technology being rolled out in 2 to 3 years is in development now. Whether it is through industry associations, your suppliers, or your network, it is important to stay plugged in to what is coming.

Ambitious goals need to be based in reality, with the people involved in setting them recognized as capable and credible. They need to understand the business well enough to set ambitious and achievable goals.

In understanding the capabilities of the organization, it is also important to understand what the organization is doing that distracts from the focus and consumes valuable resources. These actions should be eliminated to free up capacity to achieve the true goals of the organization. Examples of these items are as follows:

- Meetings and e-mail
- Production of unprofitable products
- Running inefficient equipment
- Spending time on activities that don't move the organization forward
- Initiatives that don't have clear goals, and don't support growth and efficiency

Ambitious goals make people think about what is possible, as long as they don't get overwhelmed by believing the goals are unattainable. When the direction is clear, people will start generating ideas that propel the organization forward more quickly.

To ensure that everyone was focused on the goals at Longview, we shared them at multiple levels. During monthly business reviews, every key manager discussed his or her areas and pieces of the plan to double EBITDA. It was about driving accountability, transparency, and pace.

During quarterly town hall meetings with the entire company, the goals were shared, along with progress against them.

To ensure focus was kept, the compensation program for all non-union employees was overhauled to focus on merit-based pay, and a short-term incentive plan based on making progress against the goal to double EBITA was introduced.

Remember that cascading goals sheet from Chapter 4? There was a place for long-term goals. This is where that "double EBITDA" goal would go in the Longview example. Whatever that goal is in your company, it should go there. The current-year goal would reflect the actions to be taken during the year to achieve the long-term goals.

Performance Accelerator 2: People Need to See the Path to Get There

If your organization readily launches ambitious goals, and people know there is a path and supporting capabilities to get there, they will jump on board and work toward the challenge. But if your organization doesn't typically achieve ambitious goals, they may seem unattainable when initially revealed.

Most people can't see the path from where the business is today to where it will be in the future because their view of the company doesn't allow them to see all of the pieces. When people have long tenures and haven't worked in other organizations, they may not have insight into how other businesses are achieving the types of results being contemplated.

At Longview, once the early years were passed, the perspective shifted from "We can't get there" to "What else can we do?" As you move the perspective around to what is possible, you will find more and more that you set the bar too low.

The reality is, progress toward a goal is not linear. Actions are taken, and then results jump up. It looks like Figure 7.2.

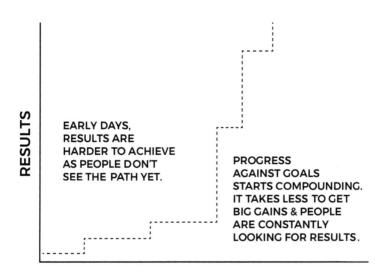

Figure 7.2 Setting the bar too low and making rapid progress

Share How the Goal Was Developed

Getting from business today to business in the future seems pretty clear to the executive team. There are typically many sessions that go into strategic and operational planning. Companies that outperform are deliberate in how the future of the business is developed. Strong insights into customer preferences and buying habits are known, the capabilities of the organization are well understood, and the path to growth has been vetted extensively.

The thing is, information is asymmetric. The executive team has lived and breathed what it takes to achieve ambitious targets. They know the steps to get there. People in middle management typically have a view of part of the plan because they have participated in putting it together. But the broader organization, many times, is largely unaware until the steps are laid out.

Steps Necessary to Get There

Let's say your organization's goal is to increase top-line revenue by 10 percent and increase earnings by 20 percent by leveraging your existing cost structure. If your market is growing at a rate of 3 percent per year, it means the other 7 percent of your revenue growth needs to come from either increasing your market share or entering new markets. Maybe the 10 percent increase seems achievable, but the bottom-line increase sounds impossible to employees without a road map.

Here's a possible road map for this example:

- You know that one of your competitors is struggling due to quality and service issues. You've identified five of its major customers whose business you have a good chance of winning.
- You have several new products that are highly desired by customers that are not yet available by your competitors.
- Your equipment is capable of running more quickly without improvements. You know you are currently running at 75 percent of the maximum capacity, and the additional volume will put you just above 80 percent of the maximum capacity. The increased volume will lower your cost per unit.

- You are adding one new piece of equipment to manufacture the new products. It is in addition to existing equipment, so you don't need to add more people. You will need to train the existing staff on the new equipment. There will be a small capital expenditure that has been included in the budget.
- You need two additional salespeople to handle the increased volume and a few additional folks in shipping and receiving.
- You are implementing automation tools to support increased volume in procuring goods, invoicing, and collections.
- You've identified multiple weekly meetings that can be consolidated or eliminated to free up time.
- You've created a short-term incentive plan for all employees that awards additional pay for the achievement of goals.

The road map clearly outlines that sales have been well thought through, the additional production is possible based on the equipment capabilities, and additional resources as outlined are necessary to achieve the targets. The money has been set aside in the annual plan, and distractions are being removed.

You may not be responsible for the entire organization, but you do have a role to play in achieving the goals for the year. By understanding how all the pieces fit together, you can have a larger impact by finding other ways to continue to grow the organization.

While this is an example of an annual goal, the same approach can be utilized to create a road map to achieving longer-term goals. The key is to outline a path that the people you lead can get around.

Performance Accelerator 3: People Need to Understand the Market and Competition

Most companies and their people don't have the benefit of massive media coverage to shed light on their relative position to competitors and provide the burning platform to support rapid progress. It is up to the leaders to highlight on a regular basis where the company stands in its competitiveness.

In the last section, we discussed one area, machine performance, where we were able to show how Longview performed against competitors.

But our conversations were much broader than that. We lagged in safety in the region. In fact, we were at the bottom, which is problematic on many levels. We shared those statistics.

From a perspective of how we compared with competitors, we showed the machine productivity graphs that put us at the bottom. We shared financial results—including EBITDA margin, cash conversion cycles, and working capital.

At the time, mills were closing around North America and the world. We showed maps of mills that were operating in Longview's space, the transportation radius of each mill, and the production capability of each mill.

The point of all this was to share where we were positioned and provide not only the road map to achieve the goals, but also the rationale for doing so.

If your business is trailing others, the business case for making rapid progress is obvious. But if your business is already outperforming its peers, it may seem like you can relax.

Top-performing leaders don't take their foot off the gas. They know if they do, a plateau will emerge, and competitors will take the lead—or the business will be disrupted.

Here's what you should be sharing with your people (your company's versus competitors' information):

- Profitability (EBITDA margin)
- Customer satisfaction ratings
- Productivity by equipment/Profitability by location
- Cost structure
- Cash conversion cycle
- Safety statistics
- Market share
- New products or services being offered
- Strategic announcements (Mergers and acquisitions, new facilities, growth initiatives, and so on)

The people you lead also need to understand who your customers are, their satisfaction with your business, and how your products or services are being used. Depending upon their position, some people will have better insight into your customers than others. After all, if you don't have customers, you don't have a business.

Here are some ways to share information about your customers with employees:

- *Share results of customer satisfaction surveys*: If done well, your customer satisfaction surveys will include insights from companies that currently do business with you, as well as companies that have elected not to do business with you. These insights will also include what they like or don't like about your competitors. This information is a road map to shoring up weak areas and emphasizing your competitive advantage. In sharing this information with employees, you should also include actions you are taking.
- *Hold a customer fair*: Depending upon your size, you may elect to do this internally or include your customers in the event. Set up a space with information about your customers and examples of how your product or service is used by your customers. This could include examples or pictures of your products. Have either customers or internal people who can talk about how your products or services are used and who uses them. While this can be done on an intranet site, having interaction and a real-life view will bring the customer experience to life for employees.
- *Share news about customers*: If you have an intranet, there should be a section dedicated to information about your customers. Information should be shared in appropriate meetings and through e-mail blasts, if critical to the operations of your business.
- *Include a customer spotlight in your newsletter*: Including stories about your customers' businesses and how you support them will make them more than an abstract concept. Your people will have a better perspective on their successes and challenges and how they play a role in both.

The people you lead need to understand the market cycles your business experiences—including the factors outside of your control that cause your business to shrink or grow. How you react to these factors is in your control, and understanding the triggers will allow you to outpace competitors.

Leading indicators inform whether your market is about to expand or contract; these will vary by industry, but there are a wide variety that are publicly available. Maybe you are impacted by housing starts or the price of oil. Understanding your leading indicators will inform you when it is time to adjust your business on the basis of market conditions.

Understanding your market, customers, and competitors will put into context how ambitious your goals are—framing up whether you are *good* or *lucky.*

Performance Accelerator 4: Celebrate Success and Remind People of Progress

People tend to lose sight of how much has been accomplished when focusing only on the path ahead. If you don't believe me, just ask people what they have accomplished in the last year or two on their own and as a department/organization. If you don't talk about it much, you'll find people are typically a bit stumped at first, then take a bit of time to come up with a fraction of what has been done.

Celebrating success is important for a number of reasons. Beyond the obvious, it helps people remember how far they have come and understand the path forward is reasonable.

Here are a few ways to celebrate success and progress:

- *Apply for awards*: As stated earlier, there are a number of awards granted by a range of industry associations, local business journals, and state associations. This isn't about pumping up the egos of the leaders. It is for the people who make the business successful. Highlighting their achievements and having them take part in the awards ceremonies engenders pride.
- *Hold milestone celebrations*: When major milestones are achieved, have a celebration to recognize the achievement in a way that is fun for people. Make sure to stress the importance of the milestone to the business.
- *Recognize significant individual and team contributions*: As discussed in the last chapter, an annual dinner that recognizes top performance in front of spouses and significant others highlights the importance of people making contributions and allows family to take part in celebrating their loved one's achievements.
- *Talk about progress in quarterly town halls*: Highlighting a list of achievements for the quarter and year reminds people of how

much progress is being made and the appreciation of their efforts. (While this was stated in the last chapter, it's important enough to revisit here in the context of celebrating success.)

Celebrating isn't just about recognizing the contributions of the people inside the company. It takes many other people beyond the walls of your business to make you successful. Don't forget to include your customers, partners, suppliers, and community members when celebrating by inviting them to major celebrations, treating them to lunch for a milestone, or sending a simple "Thank you" for smaller accomplishments.

Your Actions

By now, you've probably realized that setting expectations is not a one and done thing. It is about understanding what is possible and pushing the boundary on it. Leaders of companies that outperform find that in setting the bar on their ambitious goals, they set it too low. The good news is that running a business is a journey and not a destination. That means the bar gets raised every year (or as conditions dictate), and it will constantly adjust. Here are a few things to consider when thinking about where to set the bar:

- What actions can you take to raise the bar to stretch what is possible?
- What are your prioritized actions, and what resources do you need to accomplish them?
- What additional information can you share with people to help them see the path forward?
- How can you tighten up compensation systems to align pay and performance across the entire organization?
- What additional information can you share with employees about the market and competitors?
- What steps can you take to shed additional insights for your people into your customers' businesses?
- Do you have time set aside in the next month and quarter to celebrate success with the people you lead?
- What other gaps do you need to close after reading this chapter, and what resources do you need to close them?

CHAPTER 8

Avoiding the Plateaus and Canyons

Balancing Between Growth and Profitability

Avoiding a plateau or canyon can be one of the toughest jobs for leadership, because it requires seeing the coming declines in products or business lines and replacing them before the decline happens. It takes constant innovation and pushing past complacency and loss of focus.

Most businesses, if around long enough, will experience a plateau at some point. The response to the plateau will determine if the company resumes its growth or goes out of business. Many times, a CEO replacement is necessary to get back on track.

I want to swing back to Ford at this point, because they have gone through this cycle many times in the last two decades. Most of the trips into the canyon were a direct result of the leadership at the time; so much so that there have been six CEOs at the time of this writing in those two decades. There are several lessons from Ford that are useful to understanding what you can do in the future to avoid plateaus and landing in the canyon.

Many of Ford's current troubles started under Jacques Nasser. He was elevated to CEO in 1999. He launched an aggressive agenda to put the customer at the center of the business and expand Ford's presence by making $13 billion in acquisitions to vertically integrate and expand its brand presence.

That strategy led to a massive investment in internet and e-commerce ventures. The move challenged the relationship with the existing dealership model of selling cars. At the same time, customers were tired of existing models and were buying lighter-weight, fuel-efficient foreign models.

During Nasser's tenure, manufacturing quality slipped, as did productivity. While some say Nasser's vision for the long-term needed more time to succeed, he was focusing so much on the future that he lost sight of the day-to-day.

All of these challenges, coupled with a massive recall of Firestone tires, led to Ford losing money through multiple quarters in 2001—resulting in the ousting of Nasser after less than 2 years as CEO.

Bill Ford, Jr. succeeded Nasser. While he made some progress in unwinding the changes Nasser had made, it wasn't enough. His decision to bring Mulally on board was an important turning point that put Ford on the growth path again. You read about Mulally's success in Chapter 1, so I won't repeat it here.

But Ford stalled out again under Mulally's successor, Mark Fields. His focus drifted away from the core business; he lost focus on passenger car sales. Ford was weighed down by unprofitable business units and was spending time in global markets without having a strong foothold. Without clear priorities, warning signs were emerging internally in the company, and the board pressed Fields to sharpen its strategic focus.

With electric cars and autonomous vehicles on the horizon, Fields began to focus on this market. However, with Tesla and others in the forefront (and moving much more quickly), Ford's stock price took a heavy hit—down 40 percent in 2014.

Like Nasser, some critics suggested Fields did not have enough time to play out his long-term strategy before he departed in 2017. Neither were able to bridge the gap successfully from today to the future.

Ford's challenges with hitting plateaus, falling into canyons, and rebounding are not uncommon. Leadership has the most significant impact on how well organizations survive the ups and downs. That is why it is critical to ensure the right leader is at the helm at the right time. There are four lessons that can be learned from the successes and failures of Ford.

Pozzo Performance Accelerators:

1. Don't lose focus on the core business.
2. History repeats itself if you don't learn from it.

3. Incremental innovations need to bridge the gap between today and long-term strategies.

4. Beware of complacency and lack of external perspective.

Performance Accelerator 1: Don't Lose Focus on the Core Business

One of the hallmarks of Mulally's success at Ford was the ability to hone in on what needed to be done. He knew that Ford needed to be competitive from a productivity and cost structure perspective to compete in the world market. And he put in place a reporting structure that ensured people were focused, results were being achieved, and visibility around performance was high across the organization.

By taking this focus, Mulally was able to ensure the core business performed well. In fact, when he took the helm, he found there were so many distractions from noncore businesses that he divested them to refocus on the core.

How do you make sure you are focused on the core of the business and not getting led into left field with noncore activities or businesses? Here are a few questions to ask yourself (and other leaders):

- *What is our core business?*
- *Does it support our purpose?*
- *Why are we considering investing in other areas?*
- *Will our current customers buy the new products or services?*
- *Can we continue to focus on our core business while expanding our offerings?*
- *How will we know if it is working or not?*

With all the challenges entailed in leading a business, it is important for you to keep an eye on the core business performance. With leadership changes and focusing on strategic initiatives, acquisitions, or other needs, it is easy to let the core business be handled by an operations lead. And by taking focus off the core business to concentrate on other areas, that is typically when it begins to decline.

To stay on top of the core business, ask these questions:

- *What is working and why?*
- *What is not working and why?*
- *Do we have the right KPIs in place?*
- *Are we gaining or losing market share?*
- *How is our productivity relative to competitors?*
- *Is our quality high?*

These questions should be addressed at least monthly. In Chapter 6, KPIs were addressed. Core business KPIs need to be highlighted and reviewed weekly—and should not be consolidated with other business lines.

Why do businesses drift away from their core area of business? It is usually based on the pressure to increase earnings. Their earnings stream looks something like the one shown in Figure 8.1.

They want to minimize the impact of the down cycle, so acquisitions are made into adjacent, vertical, or cash-generating businesses that are completely unrelated.

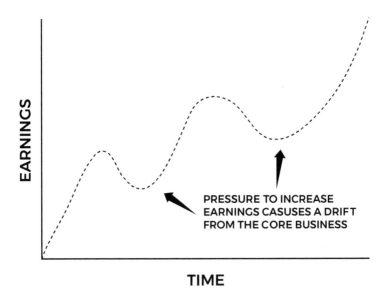

Figure 8.1 *The market cycle trap*

Jacques Nasser looked to General Electric's playbook for running Ford during his tenure. As a conglomerate, G.E. assembled a number of businesses that in many cases had nothing to do with each other. While this strategy worked for several years, G.E. is now suffering and struggling to survive.

The acquisition trend that lasted for decades to continue the earnings' growth did not allow for focus on a core business. Because the focus moved away from the core business—the industrial sector—the declines in the core business were not addressed.

A different approach to avoiding the plateaus and canyons can be taken from Jim Hackett. The oil business has historically evaluated the line where business goes from profitable to unprofitable at $40 to $50 per barrel. For a long time, it was a given that the industry would make or lose money based on the market.

In adjacent industries, the goal was to diversify to mitigate the impact of the oil cycles. Same core business, just different industries served.

But what if a different question was asked? What if, in understanding that the bottom of the market is $25 per barrel, the question becomes, "How do we make money at $35 to $45 per barrel?"

The shift in the question drives an entirely different thought process. Keeping the core business in mind, it drives thinking beyond acquisitions that are vertically driven or horizontally driven and aimed at reducing fluctuations in earnings driven by market cycles.

Performance Accelerator 2: History Repeats Itself If You Don't Learn from It

Did Fields understand the history of Ford when he took the helm in 2014? One would think yes, because he was a key leader under Nasser. In fact, he joined Ford in 1989, so he had seen the ups and downs and tenures of several of Ford's CEOs. And yet, he still made some of the same mistakes.

I've run across these types of situations across my career. A company experiences a major impact in its operations. Actions are taken to correct the situation—sometimes getting at the root cause, other times addressing the symptoms. Eventually, the trajectory of the organization changes and starts going up again.

But why doesn't the trajectory keep heading up? The most significant reason is that people are doing something new, and it hasn't become part of the culture. Here's an example of what I mean:

Business reviews were used to drive accountability, ensure goals were achieved, establish the pace, and identify roadblocks that needed to be cleared in a business I worked with. Many of the people participating had not bought into the practice and were biding their time until the CEO exited. And while the business reviews drove short-term gains, the people viewed the process as doing a required activity rather than embedding the practice into the culture.

The company also had a focus on risk identification and mitigation to avoid losses and proactively manage the business. Risks that were identified and addressed early on were no longer being sought out—leading to losses. The process of risk identification and mitigation was viewed as a corporate requirement, not an important part of the business. The practice had not become embedded in the culture.

The thing is—the people who were in the business at the time the business declined and experienced the pain of falling into the canyon are no longer there. The practices they put in place, designed to prevent similar situations, may no longer be deemed necessary years later. The new people didn't experience the pain of falling into the canyon and trying to climb out.

Successful businesses embed lessons into their culture. The oldest business on the planet is a hot spring hotel in Japan—Nishiyama Onsen Keiunkan. It was founded in 705 and has been run by the same family for 52 generations. Part of the success of the business has been due to the lessons passed from one generation to the next about hospitality and customer service that are embedded in the culture.

Unless the lessons of history are embedded in the culture of the organization, they are likely to be repeated. To embed something in your culture, people need to understand its importance and believe that acting in a different way will leave them, the customer, and the business better off. Otherwise, it just becomes an activity that people do. So, next time you want to stop doing something, it is a good idea to ask why it is being done to determine if it is no longer relevant. Otherwise, you may stop doing something that was put into place to guard against negative impacts on the business.

Performance Accelerator 3: Incremental Innovations Need to Bridge the Gap between Today and Long-Term Strategies

When the core business is running well, it is easy to take a long-term view of where the business will be in the years to come. You may think of new markets, new offerings, or new acquisitions. But, have you thought through the bridge between today and the future?

Another way to think about this is a bridge (Figure 8.2)—with each plank representing the different product or service offerings that will get you from today to the future.

Let's take the case of Mark Fields entering into the electric car market and autonomous vehicles. With the base of vehicles sold today in the gasoline/diesel passenger car category, what comes between today and the future of electric cars and autonomous vehicles?

There will be many incremental innovations that bridge from today to the future. We've covered incremental innovation in Chapter 3, so I won't repeat the information here. If you need to, go back and review to refresh your thinking on how to bridge the gap.

What you do need to consider is the disruption to your existing customers if you attempt to jump straight from today to the future. The reality is, you won't know:

- All of the innovations you will produce if the future is a long way out, or
- If the future state will turn out to be what you envision it to be today.

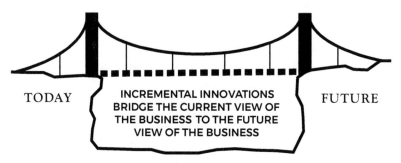

Figure 8.2 Bridging today to the future

Even if you aren't a senior leader, you play a key role in ensuring that your customers are served well today. If your organization seems to be drifting away from customers, ask about the direction. You may just find a gap that hadn't been identified previously.

The point of going through this exercise is to ensure that you don't go from a plateau to a canyon. Rather, you get off the plateau and continue to grow.

In the case of Ford under Nasser, his focus shifted from Ford's customers—dealerships—to the end customer, the ultimate buyer. The challenge with taking that leap is it erodes trust with current customers (dealerships) and disrupts the current supply chain.

During this time, the customer was no longer interested in buying the types of vehicles Ford was producing and shifted their purchasing to the lighter-weight, more fuel-efficient foreign vehicles.

At the time, many thought Nasser's perspective leveraging technology to have customers buy directly from the producer made sense. The challenge was, he missed the bridge from today to the future and ultimately lost customers.

Fields was making the same mistake in jumping straight to electric cars without bridging the gap from today to the future.

Before embarking on the journey, ask yourself (and your team) these questions:

- *Will our customers go on the journey with us?*
- *Are our current customers our future customers?*
- *If not, how do we keep our current customers satisfied while onboarding new customers?*
- *What mechanisms do we need to put in place to remain connected with customers?*
- *Do we have a path that allows customers, investors, and employees to connect the dots to our future state?*
- *What mechanisms do we have in place to alert us to innovations or strategies that are not working?*
- *Do we have enough cash to take all the steps in the journey?*

By thinking through the bridge from today to the future, you will be able to position your organization for success without losing sight of your core business.

Performance Accelerator 4: Beware of Complacency and Lack of External Perspective

When Wendy Collie took the helm at New Seasons, she found a lot of concern about growth. She knew that growth, innovation, and continuous improvement were necessary to stay relevant in a highly competitive and fast-changing industry, and build a sustainable business.

To break through the resistance to change, she created a vision that was closely tied to their mission and values. The essence was *everything healthy grows*. New Seasons is a watershed for local vendors, producers, and the regional food economy. It creates jobs and takes care of people and their families.

She contrasted the concept of the watershed with a bog. Bogs don't grow and are mainly stagnant. There is life, but what is alive is struggling to survive. A watershed in contrast becomes a fluid and dynamic environment that brings other elements into it so that everyone grows and thrives.

Wendy invited customers, community members, and vendors to a company-wide meeting to speak about how New Seasons affected their lives. Employees could see how real the watershed was, and that their neighborhood grocery store was about more than selling groceries.

This approach linked back to purpose—support local artisans, growers, farmers, and fishers strengthening the regional food economy. Grow and create jobs, and create neighborhood grocery stores that foster a thriving place for people to go and where they are part of a greater community.

By taking this approach, she was able to shift the focus out of a complacency and fear perspective and reorient the organization toward growing.

Complacency is a killer of businesses, especially after a turnaround situation like Ford experienced under Mulally. For many, it feels like a finish line has been crossed. Profits are back up, customers are pleased, and productivity is back to where it should be. *It's time to relax*, right?

That is exactly when it is time not to relax, because the rest of the world is continuing to grow and develop. By getting complacent, you allow an opening for others to fill the void.

Complacency warning indicators:

- Pace of decision making slows.
- Goals and direction are not clear.

- Incremental innovations start to decline.
- Productivity drops.
- Cost structure increases.
- Market share begins to decline.
- Customer complaints go up.
- Competitors become more active.
- Earnings plateau then decline.
- If public, stock price moves down when competitors' are going up.
- Investors and analysts start asking more questions and seem concerned.

It can be tough to see complacency starting to take hold if you are in the middle of it. But outsiders can see it. People who have insight into the operations of your competitors, or potential disruptors, can see when complacency starts creeping in.

Often, some people within the company see it happening too. They may not be those sitting at the leadership table, but they have insight that things have changed and not for the better.

So, how do you make sure that the insights about the company's performance are surfacing? Get feedback regularly from:

- Employees at all levels
- Outside board members
- Bankers and accountants
- Trusted advisors
- Customers
- Competitors

You can only get honest perspectives if you are open to them. Truth telling is an important part of culture, as it focuses on what is working and what is not. You are not merely inciting complaint sessions. Rather, you are engaging in an important part of constantly improving the business. Some cultures are not very transparent, and as a result tend not to be high-performing. No matter your level in your organization, you can drive discussions in your area.

And don't forget to watch for legislative changes that could impact your business. Mitzi Perdue experienced this situation with her rice farms in California. Legislators were considering changes that would have put her out of business.

She wrote an article explaining the rice growers' perspective and submitted it to an inflight magazine that she knew legislators would read. It became the cover article and required reading for the whole state legislature. As a result, the law was not passed.

Jim Hackett found that investors in his businesses had shifted their expectations. Years ago, they looked to 5 percent growth. But today, they look for 10 percent growth and looked at energy as an alternative to something else in the S&P 500 (which was growing at a 5 percent real growth rate). To attract capital, you have to be competitive.

Being attractive to investors forces a consideration of the asset portfolio that is necessary to have real growth over the short-term and the long-term. That growth comes from the capability to grow both organically and inorganically, depending on the market cycle.

In many of the cases discussed in this chapter, some if not many people in the business knew a hiccup was coming. Having internal people at all levels, as well as external experts, who can provide constructive feedback is critical to combating complacency and loss of focus.

Your Actions

History tells us that the likelihood of hitting a plateau or falling into a canyon is much higher than the chances of avoiding them altogether. There are ways to build mechanisms into your business by having honest assessments of what is going well and what is not.

- Are you focused on your core business? What steps do you need to take to refocus, if not?
- What actions are you taking to ensure you are not heading for a plateau or canyon?
- How are you reframing how you look at your business, so you avoid market cycles?
- What lessons are you embedding in your culture to ensure history does not repeat itself?

- What is your incremental innovation pipeline to bridge your business from today to the future?
- How do you know if you are headed in the same direction as your customers?
- What mechanisms are you putting in place to avoid complacency?
- Who are your truth tellers and early detectors of complacency?
- What other gaps do you need to close after reading this chapter, and what resources do you need to close them?

PART IV

You: Becoming a Leader— Who Is a Fine-Tuned Machine

CHAPTER 9

Elevating Your Personal Best

As a leader, to be at your best, it is important to have and maintain a high level of energy, be clear and present, and be consistent. But what does it really take for leaders to be at their best? It requires alignment between your beliefs and values, the performance of your body, and the knowledge of what works and doesn't.

Your body performs well when you are at your best, as there is an appropriate balance of exercise and nutrition that works for you. There is a consistent "you" across all facets of your life. You don't wear many masks; there is only one. You are at peace with your decisions, as they align with your values—allowing you to operate at an optimal level. And as a result, you sleep well at night.

Imagine. You are in your 70s, have a thriving business, and are a thought leader in your field. You have won multiple awards and exude more energy than people half your age. People ask you when you are going to retire. But, why would you? Life is fun, and you have a profound impact. For Alan Weiss, there is no *work life* and *personal life*. There is just *life*—a perspective he shares regularly through his books and seminars.

He has mastered the art of living holistically. And that life includes his family, his business, and his play time. Travel is balanced between family, work, and play. His days flow in a way that maximizes his impact and creates the space in his mind and body to be his best every day.

He holds degrees in political science and psychology and has worked with some of the top companies and leaders in the world. He has written 64 books, publishes prolifically, has won more awards than can be counted, and is a thought leader in his field.

Alan understands the symbiotic nature of people and business and what is necessary to constantly innovate to stay relevant. As the leader of a community of consultants, he demonstrates through action his view that to be successful, one needs to have a strong self-esteem, alignment with stated beliefs, and a healthy lifestyle to operate at one's peak. He exemplifies outperforming personal expectations.

In this chapter, we will explore the success stories of Alan Weiss—along with Abraham Lincoln. We'll also delve into past situations that caused turmoil in business. We will discuss what drove success or failure—and how you can surpass your own toughest expectations.

Why choose these two figures as focal points of this chapter, given that neither is a corporate executive? The two were/are crystal clear on their priorities and ordered/order their lives in a way that puts their priorities at the center.

In searching to find concrete examples of steps that specific executives took to embody a healthy mindset, I've found none. There are several studies, but they don't allow for drawing a straight line between actions taken and results.

Fortunately, however, there is a complete view of Lincoln that allows us to see the foundational work he did to become one of the greatest leaders in U.S. history.

As for Alan, he is the one leader I've seen successfully balance all aspects of his life to be his best every day.

A few have come pretty close to finding this balance. Many leaders I've seen and worked with have done well in some areas and not so well in other areas. They've made a series of trade-offs to advance in their careers. Alan did too. He's now in a place where he doesn't need to anymore. But, it took work to get there.

Throughout this chapter, we'll cover not only the ideal, but stories of executives who have done well on this front—and others who have not.

Pozzo Performance Accelerators:

1. You need to be clear about your personal values to lead effectively
2. To sustain a long career, you need to supercharge your energy and minimize stress
3. Resetting your perspective and having a healthy mindset is necessary to staying focused and making good decisions.

Getting Started

Becoming a great leader starts within. The foundation for achieving your personal best can be visualized as three pillars covered in this chapter: energy, mindset, and values. To maintain that focus requires a strong support system. This will be covered in Chapter 10.

As a leader, you have responsibility for the people in your company. It is no longer just about you. The more senior you are, the more impact your decisions have on their lives. How you show up every day sets the tone for the business and impacts the environment your people experience (Figure 9.1).

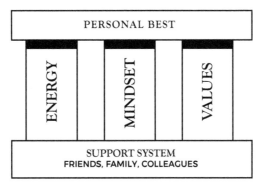

Figure 9.1 Your personal best framework

Your decisions cause the company to grow or shrink. Growing companies employ more people and have a symbiotic relationship with the community. The opposite is true when companies are in decline. Employees are often laid off and, if in a small community, may have trouble finding work. As a leader, understanding and embracing the full weight of your role is important. It requires you to be at your best, not just for you, but for your family and your people.

Performance Accelerator 1: You Need to Be Clear about Your Personal Values to Lead Effectively

Being clear about values, and the alignment of personal values with business values, is one of the biggest flashpoints for conflict—internally with an individual, between a person and the company, and between individuals in the company. The reason it is a flashpoint is values are at the heart of what is right and wrong. If values are in opposition, it creates tension—not just a disagreement about how to proceed, but fundamentally that one person is right and the other is wrong. And if values are deeply held, the reaction is typically emotional.

As this topic is gaining wider traction and focus today, many executive search firms and companies are utilizing assessment tools to ensure fit exists between executives who are being hired and the business.

Turning Points

It was early in his career that Alan formed his perspectives on living a holistic life. A few years out of college, he was looking out the window, and it struck him: he couldn't be outside and walk on the street unless it was lunch. It was not a job. It was a prison. And that scared him. With the support and consultation of his wife, he embarked on a winding journey of calculated risks and career moves that led him to his successful, thriving business today.

His journey included understanding what was important to him and putting those things at the center of his life. His family, hobbies, and helping others lead better lives topped the list. Because he is clear on his values and beliefs, they show up in what he does every day. There is no space between his personal values and business values.

This may seem like an extreme approach to aligning values between the individual and a business. It is true that many do not fully step out of corporate life to start their own businesses. But Alan's move to a different career shows a thoughtful approach to finding a good fit based on values.

You've probably worked with people who didn't seem to "fit" in your business, or you may have had times when you felt like you didn't "fit." Take a minute to think about why that was. What was important to you, and what was important to the business?

Finding Your Values

Because there is a symbiotic relationship between the leaders of a company and the company itself, it is critical for the values of the company and its leaders to be clear and aligned. Having clear alignment means that when actions are taken, they are understandable and reflect the underlying values. In other words, the values manifest in behaviors that advance the organization. This is typically transparent throughout the organization and creates a level of trust and respect.

Values inform behaviors and actions. They are at the core of why you act the way you act. But values aren't typically chosen; they emerge based on each individual's background. People believe what they see. Actions need to be aligned with stated beliefs. That is why it is so important that as a leader, you are clear about your values.

Think back to times in your life when you had strong reactions, both positive and negative. The strong positive reactions are generally times when there was a strong alignment with your values. The strong negatives were likely at times when something was in conflict with your values. Ask yourself *why*, over and over, until you get to the core of what specifically was causing a strong reaction in you. That will get to your core values.

If you haven't already done so, take the time to write down your core values. Table 9.1 lists a few examples of core values.

Once you determine your core values, write them down and post them where you can see them every day.

The example in Table 9.2 is designed to keep you focused on your values through quarterly check-ins. It is helpful to gain unvarnished insights from others to ensure that your perspective on how you are living your

Table 9.1 Sample core values

Acceptance	Achievement	Adventure	Balance
Beauty	Boldness	Compassion	Challenge
Community	Contribution	Creativity	Curiosity
Fairness	Faith	Friendships	Fun
Growth	Happiness	Honesty	Humor
Inner Harmony	Kindness	Knowledge	Leadership
Learning	Love	Loyalty	Meaningful Work
Openness	Optimism	Peace	Recognition
Religion	Reputation	Respect	Responsibility
Security	Self-Respect	Service	Success
Status	Trustworthiness	Wealth	Wisdom

Table 9.2 Personal values worksheet

Personal Values Worksheet (list 4–5)		
Value 1	Value 2	Value 3
Value 4	Value 5	
Quarterly Values Alignment Check-In		
Am I living my values at work and at home?		
Value 1		
Value 2		
Value 3		
Value 4		
Value 5		
Would my friends and family agree?		
Value 1		
Value 2		
Value 3		
Value 4		
Value 5		
What changes are needed, and how will I hold myself accountable?		
Value 1		
Value 2		
Value 3		
Value 4		
Value 5		

values is in alignment with how others are experiencing you. Just make sure you ask the right people—those who want to help you grow and know you—not just anyone.

The strongest leaders manifest their values. Those values show up in their actions every day. By checking in on your values, you'll be able to pinpoint any gaps that may be creeping into your life and work culture.

Jim Hackett noticed that many of the struggles others experienced were because they had intellectualized their sense of values as *good* or *bad*. There was no heart and soul, no spirituality in incorporating values. As a result, when challenges arose, self-interest crept in and led to bad decisions.

Performance Accelerator 2: To Sustain a Long Career, You Need to Supercharge Your Energy and Minimize Stress

When Stress Wreaks Havoc

It was April 19, 2004. A gathering of 14,000 people from around the world convened in Orlando, Florida, for a biannual meeting of McDonald's franchisees. What was about to happen would ripple through the organization and business community.

Sixteen months before the international franchisee meeting, James Cantalupo was brought out of retirement to serve in the chief executive role and revitalize the company. He was widely credited for growing the international presence of McDonald's before he retired, solidifying its position. For the first time ever, McDonald's posted a quarterly loss. Its former chief executive was forced out by investors and franchise owners. Sales and service had to be addressed quickly.

Having come out of retirement and approaching 60, Cantalupo was cognizant of the need for a succession plan that would allow for years of grooming to ready his successor. Charlie Bell was selected. He had grown up in the company, flipping burgers in Australia at 15. He worked his way up through the organization, being tapped as heir apparent to Cantalupo at the age of 42.

With the pressure of sliding earnings and stock prices, and the close eye of investors and franchise owners who had forced Cantalupo's predecessor out, the timeline to transform the organization was short. The results came quickly. The menu was adjusted to address a more health-conscious consumer desire, and service levels began to tick up.

People familiar with the organization commented on the transformation of Cantalupo himself. After being overweight in the 1990s, he had become fit. His lifestyle was a challenge though. His international travel schedule was heavy, which for many, in combination with the pressure of a major transformation, results in high stress.

At 5:00 a.m. on April 19, 2004, just hours before he was to share the success of the transformation, Cantalupo suffered a massive heart attack that resulted in his death at the age of 60. All the top leaders and directors were in attendance for the meeting. By 6:45 a.m., Bell was immediately elevated to the top role. He was 43 years old and expected to serve in that role for many years to come.

It was about that time that Bell was suffering from stomach pains. Three weeks into his tenure as chief executive, exploratory surgery revealed he had colorectal cancer. Nine months later, in January 2005, Bell passed away at age 44.

Both losses had profound impacts on the company and families of the men who passed away at young ages. These are unusual examples of major health issues that were both highly publicized and in close proximity to each other. Having to appoint three CEOs in the space of a year and a half raised the touchy issue of the health of leaders that are integral to the success of an organization.

More than a decade later, on October 15, 2015, Oscar Munoz was 37 days into his tenure at United Airlines when his legs gave out, he became clammy, and he suffered a devastating heart attack. He crawled to the landline phone and called 911. It was early in the morning and other people were not around. He knew that cell phones didn't show locations and that using a landline would alert responders to his location.

Munoz had been brought into United to turn around the struggling airline after its former chief executive was forced to resign amidst a corruption scandal. It was struggling with completing the merger with Continental Airlines, technology glitches, and poor customer service. Munoz had embarked on a listening tour, flying on cramped regional jets and hearing the complaints of people around the country.

The circumstances of Munoz's heart attack are a bit unusual. He was a vegan and exercised regularly. At 56 years old, his exercise regime included bike riding, golf, and tennis. It was during his morning exercise that the heart attack struck. His quick action of calling 911 allowed him to survive after a heart transplant, and likely, so did his general health.

The information on the health and lifestyles of the three men is not generally available. These situations were extreme, but so too were the circumstances in their businesses. It is a reminder to step back and reflect on the relationship between stress and health. Among the top 10 health problems associated with stress are heart disease and premature death. These cases also highlight the impact on the business when top leaders suffer from major health issues.

The lesson for you as an individual is to monitor your stress levels and build in stress-relieving activities on a daily basis. In the midst of turmoil, it is hard to accurately assess the impact of stress on oneself. Having someone who can tell you when you are exhibiting the effects of high stress and push you to address it is important. In Chapter 10, we cover building a personal board of directors. Having one of your directors focused on this (which we will discuss later) is important.

There is a tricky line to walk between businesses and individuals, as health information is private and is a sensitive topic. However, if you are responsible for hiring people who will be leading the entire business or a portion of your business, understanding how they handle stress is important. Many assessments today attempt to address how stress is handled.

Separately, in conversations, asking questions about what actions people take to handle stress on a daily basis is important. You'll learn a lot about how self-aware people are and how they address stressful times.

You and Your Energy

The personal energy necessary to sustain peak performance personally—and as a leader of a company—requires constant renewal. Finding daily, weekly, and monthly time-outs to recenter and fill up the energy bank, rather than depleting it, is critical to sustaining peak performance. As important as managing your time is managing your energy and minimizing stress. The following five key areas are necessary to achieve optimal energy while minimizing stress:

- Figure out who and what energizes and drains you.
- Get enough good sleep at night.
- Eat what works for your body.
- Exercise regularly.
- Work with your natural rhythms to the extent you can.

Profile in Success

Alan Weiss (Table 9.3) has mastered a holistic approach to life that allows him to maximize his energy. His laser-like focus allows him to quickly

Table 9.3 Profile in success: Alan Weiss

Day Starts	6 a.m.
Work Ends	2 p.m.
Hobbies	Building models, reading, travel, wine, exotic cars, theater
Typical meeting duration	15 minutes
Responds to e-mail and voice mail	Every 1.5 hours for 15 minutes
E-mail inbox	Empty at the end of the day
Exercise	Personal trainer 3× week for an hour
Sleep	5–6 hours
Diet	Small meals frequently, dinner out 7 days a week
Vacation	Scheduled first—work scheduled to integrate with vacation
High-energy time	Morning
Breaks	Afternoon
Tips for success	You have one life, not a work life and a personal life. Integrate them
	Learn to say no

move through his day, spending and recharging his energy in a manner such that he is always at the top of his game.

Alan has mastered the flow of his energy. He knows his natural rhythms. His high-energy time is in the morning and he performs his high-concentration activities then. In the afternoon, he builds models and does other activities that restore his energy. He gets enough good sleep at night and feels rested when he gets up. Exercise strengthens his body and clears his mind, reducing stress levels.

Alan was not always able to take this approach. Early in his career, he traveled much more exclusively for work and was not able to integrate his family as much. Over the years, he constantly reinvented himself in a way that allowed him to reach his ideal state that you see today.

Take a few minutes to plug your information into this matrix. How does yours compare? What do you notice? Are your meeting durations substantially longer? Are you getting exercise? How can you trim time busters to create time for things that matter to you?

There are ways to free up your time so that you can go to your child's play or game. You may schedule time at lunch to exercise, or in the morning before work. The point is to take deliberate steps to schedule in the things that are most important to you.

The Energy Roller Coaster

Energy ebbs and flows throughout the day and can be impacted by when and what you eat, how you exercise, the intensity of interactions, etc. Sometimes your energy can seem like a roller coaster. Finding out what works best for you in terms of the types of activities and your energy is important to using your energy wisely.

For example, if you need to concentrate on an issue that requires deep thought, morning may be the best time. Walking around and talking to people to get a pulse of the organization may be best done on Friday after lunch, as people are mentally winding down. The point is to work with the natural flow of your energy to operate at your peak.

The Lunch Cacophony

We were all fairly new to Longview, and lunch was a time when we could get together. Pizza kept showing up. In an attempt to be healthier, the meals started shifting to sandwiches. The meeting length began to vary, as did the topics—starting in the morning with a brief lunch break, then resuming for the afternoon.

Being noise sensitive, I started to notice that about a third of the people in the room would cough for about an hour after lunch—a cacophony of phlegmy coughs. Varying the lunch made a difference. When we had a salad bar that was low on gluten and dairy, the level of coughing decreased. On sandwich bar days, it increased.

The people I tipped off were shocked as they listened to the room before and after lunch. If you asked people in the room, most would say they did not have any issue with food. But clearly, many did.

Conversely, I've been to meetings where the room was silent after lunch. In those cases, people talked while going through the buffet line about what they did and did not eat based on their preferences and what worked for them. They were all aware of what worked for them and didn't. And based on the noise level, clearly, they were right.

Different foods work for different people. Go to any bookstore, and you will find a plethora of books on what to eat or not eat based on the latest study. There are perspectives based on body type, blood type, health issues (heart, autoimmune, etc.), and many others. I'm not a doctor, so I would always recommend that you talk to a professional on this topic before making radical changes. For a number of folks and for me, the best result came from working with a naturopath to test for food allergies and intolerances. It is pretty amazing to find out how much food impacts how you feel and your energy level every day.

The Energizer Bunny versus Dracula

Have you ever thought about how you feel after various interactions and experiences? Sometimes you feel like the Energizer bunny, because the interaction really got you pumped up. Other times, you feel like Dracula just sucked the life out of you. Some people really enjoy being in a crowd. For others, being in a crowd is draining. Maybe you drive down the street and enjoy the scenery, while others get frustrated sitting in traffic. Meetings, colleagues, friends, family, events, etc., will elicit a response from you that either excites or drains you. Table 9.4 lists an example worksheet that can help you track your energy. Add or subtract topics based on your own observation and reflection. Then spend less time with the people or activities that drain you and more time with the people and activities that energize you.

Table 9.4 Energy tracking sheet

	Impact on energy	
	Energizes	**Drains**
Large parties or meetings		
Making small talk		
One-on-one conversations		
Quiet time		
Meetings		
Debating the topic of the day		
Meeting new people		
Interruptions		
Juggling multiple priorities		

Performance Accelerator 3: Resetting Your Perspective and Having a Healthy Mindset Are Necessary to Staying Focused and Making Good Decisions

A Nation on the Brink

Little is written about the depths of the inner mind of contemporary business leaders. The actions taken and leadership philosophies are the subject of a plethora of articles and books. But, we don't get insight into their inner thoughts. To gain insight into the strength, humility, and self-reflection of truly successful leaders requires the ability to review diaries, correspondence, and insights of contemporaries.

Abraham Lincoln has been the subject of much examination in the century and a half since his death. Time has allowed for a holistic picture of the man and the leader. His writings have provided an insight into the development of his mindset and perspective over the course of his life.

Lincoln experienced melancholy throughout his life. Some have viewed this as depression. Others view it as part of his nature, a source of creativity and achievement. For Lincoln, it presented the opportunity for deep reflection. He exposed his fears and spoke openly—not only with doctors and family, but also with colleagues. He was able to leverage his fears to focus on his desire to accomplish something during his life.

He explored the psychology of the time, working to understand himself, improve himself, exercise discipline, and develop strategies to navigate the hard times. This was the foundation of his character. He understood deeply what was driving him and how to be deliberate about his actions.

It was from his early days of struggle that he learned how to read people and situations and shape events to achieve the outcomes he desired. This was clear when his competitors failed to achieve the nomination for presidency, and he prevailed. But this came only after he lost two bids for the U.S. Senate. His frame of mind was not that of failure, but of what could be done to achieve success next time.

He was able to see through the slights, disdain, and opposition of his rivals. His strong mental discipline allowed him to dismiss them internally and move on to productive matters. He saw their strengths and how their talents could steer the country through a troubled time. His own sense of humility and persistence won over his rivals one by one, starting with Seward.

Renowned for his sense of humor and gift for storytelling, Lincoln was able to lighten the mood when tensions rose—and lift spirits. His work early in his life provided him with an even-tempered and clear view of situations, allowing him to shift his own moods and provide stability for his team.

It was Lincoln's self-knowledge and ability to regulate himself that allowed him to be an effective leader. His strong sense of self allowed his ego to remain in check, so he could take the actions necessary to hold the country together.

The Building Blocks of a Healthy Mindset

Leadership can be tough. It also can be fun. It requires hard choices. It also requires calculated risks. To be effective, it requires you to be in a good place personally. Self-reflection is crucial to learning and growing and making effective decisions. Leading an organization requires a strong sense of self, emotional health, and openness to different perspectives.

Given the symbiotic relationship between an organization and its leaders, it takes a healthy leader to have a healthy organization. Here's what you need to do to find your building blocks:

- Get to the bottom of what drives you.
- Choose to be happy.
- Fail forward.
- See through actions to intentions.
- Surround yourself with positive people.
- Clear the mind.
- Have fun and laugh.

Lincoln is arguably the clearest example of the interrelationship between leadership and those he was leading. The past informs the future. It is a simple concept, but one that is not often considered from a personal perspective. Leaders unconsciously bring fears and behaviors rooted in childhood patterns and experiences into the business environment. These behaviors manifest as controlling activities, lack of trust, and inability to delegate. Few leaders have gone to the depths of Lincoln to achieve

Table 9.5 Daily mindset check-in

	Yes	No
Did I do my best today to have a positive outlook?		
Did I understand what was driving my reactions?		
Did I have fun and laugh today?		
Did I do my best today to give people the benefit of the doubt?		
Did I learn from my failures and setbacks today?		
Did I let the little stuff go and move forward?		

self-awareness. Those who have done so have tended to lead their organizations to a higher level of success.

Holding Yourself Accountable

Change only happens with constant focus and mechanisms to keep you on track every day. The best way to do that is ask yourself a series of questions at the end of the day to check in on your mindset. Marshall Goldsmith does this every day and has made progress on his personal goals because of it.

An example shown in Table 9.5 can be changed to suit your needs. The asking of questions is best done by someone else, as the tendency will be to defer to a later date. You won't want to say no. If you stick with it, you'll start thinking about what you need to do to say yes.

Your Actions

Achieving your personal best requires mastering your energy, mindset, and values. Leaders who do this consistently position themselves and their companies to outperform expectations. Following are key highlights from the chapter:

- What actions can you take to remove the barriers between your work and personal life that create conflicts?
- How can you address gaps, if any, between your personal values and the values of your business?

- What actions do you need to maximize energy?
- What additional support do you need to reduce stress?
- What changes do you need in order to have a healthy mindset?
- What other gaps do you need to close after reading this chapter, and what resources do you need to close them?

CHAPTER 10

Developing Your Knights of the Roundtable

Imagine King Arthur sitting around a roundtable with his key advisors giving him extraordinary advice. While this scene may be more from a movie than real life, it is a sound point. Successful people get advice from other successful people, not just in business, but also in life.

If you think about the construction of a corporate board of directors, it will include people with strengths in varying areas of business and different industries, if it is constructed well. They provide insights, challenge direction and strategy, and drive accountability. And they will all be really good at what they do.

Now take that to a personal level. What would your life look like if you were deliberate in creating a personal board of directors to help you be successful? We've covered a lot of ground in this book so far. Where are your gaps? What do you want to learn and focus on, both professionally and personally?

All of the people I interviewed for this book have sought advice over the course of their careers. They have people who they can speak with about certain topics—to seek advice and challenge their thinking. They have all developed relationships over their lifetimes that are appropriate for each point in time.

As they've grown, they've developed new relationships with people who can challenge them at each stage of their careers and lives. They've recognized that the insights and understanding of the demands change.

While each would not claim to be deliberate in building a personal board of directors, you'll find a deliberateness in seeking out advice and creating conditions for holding one's self accountable.

Many times, people know they need help staying on track, and they pay people to help them stay the course. Like many executives, Alan Weiss hires a personal trainer to stay on track with his exercise program. Marshall Goldsmith hires a person to keep him on track with his personal commitments.

Alan Mulally held himself accountable with his family by using a weekly review process where he and his family went through the family goals for the week. The process forced him to make his personal and family goals a priority.

What they all have done in an informal manner is create a personal board of directors. They have people who push them, share insights, and hold them accountable. And they have changed those board members over time based on shifting circumstances.

There are three performance accelerators we can take away from these successful leaders about how to create and utilize a personal board of directors.

Pozzo Performance Accelerators:

1. Design your personal board of directors that sets you up to outperform.
2. Establish your personal goals.
3. Enroll your directors.

Successful people get advice from other successful people, not just in business, but also in life. A personal board of directors helps you keep focused on your personal goals and objectives, resulting in a fulfilling life. They challenge you. They push you to achieve your personal best. And they hold you accountable when you aren't focused on the things that you claim are a priority. While you will always have family members who can give you a perspective, it is important to have people outside your family circle and business to broaden your perspective.

Performance Accelerator 1: Design Your Personal Board of Directors That Sets You up to Outperform

As you think about building your personal board of directors, there are several "seats" that should be filled. A number of these can be filled by paying an advisor or coach. Others may be filled by people you respect. Here's a few you should consider:

- *Career advice*: Throughout your career, you will need to learn new skills, develop internal and external networks, and have people who help you advance in your roles. You may have several people who fill this role to challenge you on what you are doing well and fill gaps necessary to have a successful career.

  Back when I was at Fluor, a coworker and I mapped out what was necessary to advance our careers, in terms of both education and experience. He and I were both in mid-career and thinking about our career growth. We continued to bounce ideas off each other for a few years. It was a great exercise, and one I've found is not deliberately undertaken enough.

- *Business advice*: There will be challenges in your business from time to time that require you to seek advice external to your company. Absolute confidentiality and depth of experience are necessary when seeking advice.

  Each of the leaders I spoke with reflected that they had people they spoke with at different times in their career. I've observed many successful people reaching out to others to inform their decision making. They aren't just looking for "yes" people. They want their thinking to be challenged. And thus, the people who they are looking to for advice must be similarly situated in their careers. Conversely, the folks I've observed struggling to make their businesses survive want to do it all themselves and don't seek out good advice.

- *Liberal arts*: Fundamental to the liberal arts is *first principle thinking*. A first principle is the foundation. If you are trying to work a problem, you have to go to the foundation to find the solution; it requires a logical process. There is a basis in logic and perspective that many times is not taught as part of a business education. Having people who are steeped in the liberal arts will challenge your thinking and provide a different perspective.

  You may be scratching your head on this one. Through the course of conversations about this book with successful leaders in the business community, this topic came up more than I would have expected. Leaders who have both business and liberal arts educations credit their liberal arts education with giving them a broader and more strategic perspective.

Stephen Babson believes a grounding in the humanities leads to a broader perspective, the ability to communicate with and relate to people on a deeper level, and a broader appreciation for the issues of the day. This grounding also leads to pattern recognition—the ability to spot trends and patterns across a wide array of conditions.

- *Philanthropy*: Philanthropy is a highly personal subject. Many people provide time and money as they become more successful in their careers. But not all philanthropic endeavours are equal. Understanding organizational effectiveness is important. Having a trusted perspective with no skin in the game is helpful in determining where to give back.

Becoming involved in philanthropy at some level is something many leaders find grounding. The higher you move in an organization and the more financially successful you become, the farther away from the daily struggles of life you become.

The most successful leaders I spoke with felt part of their success enabled them to give back to the community in areas where they had a passion. They all had a common view about ensuring their contributions went toward the mission, not overhead. They deliberately evaluated the impact of the organizations they supported. And many times they had a neutral perspective in making that evaluation. Accessible to everyone is Charity Navigator. More sophisticated and wealthy individuals have personalized, typically hired, support in making their decisions.

- *Personal financial advice*: The point of financial planning is to ensure you have the lifestyle you want when you retire. If you plan to retire at 60 and expect to live until 85 or 90, that is 25 to 30 years of income to cover. The key to this is to start early and assign someone to keep you on track.

Surprised to see this one here? Most people think they are on track financially until they are about to retire. Divorces, kids in college, medical emergencies, etc., have a way of derailing many people. Retirement has been delayed years for a number of executives I know, because finances were not in the right place to support their lifestyle.

- *Physical well-being*: Getting daily exercise can become a challenge with all of the pulls on your time. It is much easier to get to the gym, take a walk or run, or do an exercise video if you have others doing it with you.

  The most successful executives who do well in this arena have a level of commitment to a person or group of people. Some have a personal trainer. Others have a team exercise, like basketball, baseball, or soccer. Still others have a group class they take where relationships have been developed. There is a level of accountability to the trainer or group that causes them to keep going.

- *Emotional well-being*: Life has high and low points. When you hit a tough patch, who can you reach out to for support? Having this relationship is important before it is needed.

  The most successful leaders I've seen have a support network that kicks into gear when major life events happen. Usually there are many who provide support at different levels and from different aspects. For some, church plays a role. Close relationships at the gym allow for stress relief. Individual friends play varying roles—from meals and lodging to a shoulder to cry on. They also push the person not to wallow, but to come to grips quickly and move on in life.

- *Positivity*: You know those people who are great to be around because they are always upbeat? You may be one and have an unlimited source of positivity. If you aren't, make sure you have people in your life who are and spend time with them.

  A consistent theme with all the successful leaders I've observed is a positive outlook. They are deliberate in creating a positive mindset every day. They don't spend time with people who are constantly negative. They cut them out of their sphere. They consistently spend time with people who are positive in their outlook. That doesn't mean they aren't realistic. It means they enjoy life and look forward to living it.

- *Accountability Partner*: Marshall Goldsmith has shared one of his secrets to making progress on things that are important to him, such as spending time with his family. His secret is having someone who calls him every day to ask him five or six questions. They are yes or no questions, and the call takes no more than 5 minutes, but it keeps his priorities front and center.

Each of these considerations may or may not fit with what you find important today and for your future. The great thing about a personal board is you can add or subtract at any time. The key point is you have a support system to help you achieve your goals and stay focused and balanced in your life.

Performance Accelerator 2: Establish Your Personal Goals

At different stages of life, you will have different priorities. As a leader in your business, it is important that you feel satisfied and whole in your personal life in order to be effective at work. You only have one life, and how you feel about each aspect of your life will affect how you show up.

As you think about your personal goals (which may include a professional component), consider the questions on the worksheet in Table 10.1:

Table 10.1 Your focused personal goals

	What is the goal?	How will it be measured?	Why is it important to you?	What support do you need?
Goal #1				
Goal #2				
Goal #3				

You shouldn't have more than three significant goals at any given time, as more than that will draw your focus away from real priorities. Goals may include:

- Getting a promotion
- Running a larger business
- Spending more time with family
- Starting a family

- Retiring in the next 5 years
- Improving your personal financial position
- Losing weight
- Adopting a healthier lifestyle
- Learning about other cultures or places

These goals should fit in with your long-term priorities—the stepping stones to get you to where you want to be.

These goals are the basis for your focus for the year—and the driver for who to engage as part of your personal board. As you share your short- and longer-term perspectives, you may find that you don't have the right goals for the near-term to accomplish your longer-term perspectives.

Having an open mind and willingness to be challenged by your personal board of directors are important to having a successful relationship. The board should be there to push you to grow—which requires you to adjust your approach to be successful.

Performance Accelerator 3: Enroll Your Directors

You will accomplish what you make a priority. It is an easy concept, but hard to implement and really embrace. But once you do, your personal board of directors can help you stay on track. Here are a few characteristics to consider when selecting your board members:

Who Will Challenge Your Thinking?

It is really easy to surround yourself with people who think like you and agree with your perspectives. That doesn't help you grow. Who in your circle has a different viewpoint that is at odds with yours? Who stretches your thinking by getting you to see possibilities you hadn't realized existed?

Who Inspires You to Grow?

These people may or may not be working in your current business. They see the potential in you and challenge you to develop your skills.

They understand your passion and challenge you to be your best. They push you to align your values with what you do every day. They inspire you to become your best self.

Who Will Call B.S. When You Start Making Excuses?

You do many things well. And some things not so well. Who knows you well enough to give you an unvarnished, helpful perspective? There may be two people—one at work and one in life. Build on your strengths, and shore up your weaknesses. It is important to be specific on the areas that need help, and not to generalize them. Conversely, generalizing strengths is appropriate. Who can you recruit to give you a frank and constructive perspective?

Who Is Trustworthy?

You can never guarantee absolute confidentiality and must be careful not to reveal sensitive information in your conversations. But, the people you are enrolling as personal board members should have high character and not repeat conversations you have with them.

Imagine a board table with 10 to 12 seats around it. Half should be people that can give you professional advice and the other half, personal advice. Each of the seats represents a role you would like represented on your personal board. It may look like the one shown in Figure 10.1:

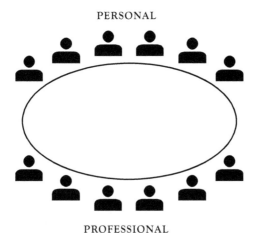

Figure 10.1 Your personal board of directors

When thinking about who should fill each seat, you may want to consider a few candidates, as your first choice may not have the capacity to serve on your personal board at this time. The selections should have the characteristics previously described. Here's a worksheet that can help you think through your selections (Table 10.2):

Table 10.2 Your personal board of directors slate of candidates

	Seat 1: Career Advice	Seat 2: Career Advice	Seat 3: Business Advice	Seat 4: Business Advice
Candidate #1				
Candidate #2				
Candidate #3				

You should also think through how much time you are going to ask of them. Is it an hour per quarter over lunch or dinner? A periodic phone call for 10 minutes? Be thoughtful in how much time you ask for.

When you engage your personal board of directors, invite them to participate on your personal board. Explain your goals, why you are reaching out to them, and what role you would like them to play—and make sure they are OK with all of it. When they fill that role, make sure you are ready for conducting the board meetings. Time is a limited resource, so you should be fully engaged when you are working with your personal board of directors. There should be something in it for them. Buy them lunch or dinner, or provide support to them in other ways. And don't forget to express your appreciation.

The seats on your board may change over time, as you grow and your life changes. Relationships will naturally run their course and conclude. New needs will arise that may drive the need for new directors.

Your Actions

The most successful people have coaches, mentors, and a support system. They may not officially call this a personal board of directors, but they have one nonetheless. Do you want to accelerate your success by creating a personal board of directors? Here are some questions to consider:

- What seats do you need to fill on your board based on your current goals?
- How are you finding blind spots and getting advice to avoid them?
- Why did you not fill certain seats (because focusing on it is too hard, or is it actually not needed now)?
- Who is your accountability partner?
- How will you respond when you get pushed by your accountability partner?
- What actions are you taking to enroll your directors?
- Who are your board candidates?
- What is in it for them to be on your board?
- What other gaps do you need to close after reading this chapter, and what resources do you need to close them?

CHAPTER 11

Charting Your Path Forward

We've covered a lot of ground through this book in looking at what it takes to outperform in your business and as a leader. If you've completed every exercise and answered every question, you have a list of actions to take. The trick now is to prioritize the actions, so you get the biggest gains quickly.

Let's look back at the High-Performing Index (Table 11.1) you completed in Chapter 1. A good place to start is where you checked *no*.

Table 11.1 The high-performing index

Chapters		Yes	No
2	Every person in your business can explain what your business is about (your purpose).		
5	You are constantly being asked by customers, industry associations, publications, and advisors to speak and for tours of your facility.		
7	Your earnings are in the top 10 percent of your industry.		
2, 4	Your people are constantly being sought by other businesses, and they choose to stay with you.		
4	Your people work collaboratively across the organization to further your goals.		
4	You have healthy debate when making decisions, varying perspectives are shared, and a decision is made and acted on quickly.		
3	New products are constantly being innovated and introduced.		
5	Your customers are so pleased by your goods or services, they actively recommend them to others.		
6	You regularly share your goals and expectations, as well as how your organization is performing.		
7	Your expectations are high, and you know your people are capable of achieving your goals.		

(continued)

Table 11.1 The high-performing index (continued)

Chapters		Yes	No
8	Your earnings are constantly growing, and the dips mirror market swings and are not a loss of market share or declining margins.		
9	Your energy is high, and you are excited to go to work every day.		
10	You have a group of people who inspire you and who will give you frank perspectives and advice when you need it.		

Go back to the chapter that relates to where you checked *no*, and take a look at the answers to the questions in that chapter. Those are likely the areas that need prioritization first (Table 11.2). In addition, consider the following:

- What is important to you?
- What will have the most impact?
- Based on your responses, pick the top three to focus on first.

Table 11.2 Performance priorities

Action	Measure of success	Resources needed	When it will be completed

Don't let the other items fall from your attention. As soon as you complete one of your top three, move the next most important onto the list. For anything you noted as unimportant, drop it from the list.

With deliberate action, you will be outperforming soon. And don't forget to revisit regularly to make sure you stay there!

APPENDIX A

Road Map to Being High-Performing

The following road map brings all of the concepts throughout the book together into one easy-to-reference place. This appendix and the results from Chapter 11 serve as a cheat sheet to staying focused on the right things on a daily basis.

Building blocks	Implications	Performance accelerators	High performers
Part I: Purpose and Relevance: Why Your Business Exists and How to Evolve to Stay Relevant			
Purpose (Chapter 2)	People need to know your company's purpose, what you are about. A clear purpose aligns people around what the company is about and who and how to attract ideal customers, investors, and employees.	• Your purpose needs to be clear and unambiguous. • Your purpose should be at the center of everything you do. • Your purpose needs to resonate with customers. • Your employees should share a passion for your purpose. • Profit and purpose don't need to be at odds.	Facebook, TOMS, Longview, EY, Wendy Collie, Tom Hellie/ Linfield
Innovation (Chapter 3)	Businesses that don't innovate go out of business.	• Disruptive innovation comes from a friction point that completely changes the way a product or service is delivered. • When a new business model/ method of delivery has been established, innovation becomes incremental and focused on making things better. • Your culture needs to reward thoughtful experiments and idea generation in order to innovate.	Netflix, Airbnb, Benjamin Franklin, Mitzi Perdue, Apple, Brian Ferriso, Jim Hackett, Linfield

(continued)

(continued)

Building blocks	Implications	Performance accelerators	High performers
Part II: Your Team Extends beyond the Four Walls of the Business			
Team (Chapter 4)	Having top talent that works together will propel your business forward farther and faster.	• Acquire the right skills and capabilities, and avoid critical mistakes. • Drive the business with top talent—in the right place. • Find the balance of people who have been in the organization and people new to the organization. • Create a direct line of sight for each person to the overarching goals. • Bust through resistance and conflict. • Get rid of friction points that drive top performers from your business.	Jim Hackett, Stephen Babson, Wendy Collie, Longview, Mitzi Perdue
Your Following (Chapter 5)	People will tell everyone they know what they think of your business. Make it count.	• Give customers what they value. • Put the customer first; don't let the process drive bad decisions. • Create situations where your people and your customers can be your evangelists.	Amazon, Longview, Nordstrom, Multnomah Athletic Club, Alan Weiss, New Seasons, Mitzi Perdue, Brian Ferriso/PAM
Part III: Keeping Score and Reaching New Heights			
Scoreboard (Chapter 6)	Keeping track of the right metrics will drive the right decisions and focus on results.	• Define success, related targets, and key performance indicators. • Report against targets regularly. • Hold people accountable for achieving results. • Create multiple channels to share targets across the organization.	Longview, Ford, Stephen Babson, Brian Ferriso/PAM, Jim Hackett, Mitzi Perdue

Building blocks	Implications	Performance accelerators	High performers
High Expectations (Chapter 7)	Setting your bar high will cause people to think about what is possible.	• Goals should be ambitious, known to everyone, and the center of focus. • People need to see the path to get there. • People need to understand the market and competition. • Celebrate success and remind people of progress.	Longview, Stephen Babson
Avoid Plateaus (Chapter 8)	There is no finish line. Celebrate milestones along the way, while challenging yourself to get better.	• Don't lose focus on the core business. • History repeats itself if you don't learn from it. • Incremental innovations need to bridge the gap between today and long-term strategies. • Beware of complacency and lack of external perspective.	Ford, Nishi-yama Onsen Keiunkan, Wendy Collie, Mitzi Perdue, Jim Hackett
Part IV: You: Becoming a Leader—Who Is a Fine-Tuned Machine			
Your Best (Chapter 9)	You need to be at your personal best to lead an organization to achieve its best.	• You need to be clear about your personal values to lead effectively. • To sustain a long career, you need to supercharge your energy and minimize stress. • Resetting your perspective and having a healthy mindset are necessary to staying focused and making good decisions.	Alan Weiss, Abraham Lincoln, Jim Hackett
Personal Advisers (Chapter 10)	Strong leaders have people they surround themselves with to challenge them to grow.	• Design your personal board of directors that sets you up to outperform. • Establish your personal goals. • Enroll your directors.	The accomplished leaders that lent their insights in the aggregate.

APPENDIX B

Reports Compendium

The following is a compendium of reports that you would typically expect to see in a manufacturing environment. Some of the reporting would apply to any type of business. If you are not in a manufacturing business, imagine what you might need in real-time, daily, weekly, or monthly based on the descriptions for each section.

While you may be in a different industry, it is helpful to see a comprehensive view of the reporting necessary to achieve desired results. You can use this information as a guide to creating or filling in the gaps for your own comprehensive reporting structure.

Real-Time

These reports are typically associated with operations and let frontline people know if they are producing at the pace necessary to achieve the expected results for the day. A few examples are:

- *Production rates/machine speeds*: This type of report is typically built into production equipment and shows the target rate for production versus the actual rate. It lets the operators know to speed up or if they are on track.
- *Throughput*: This signal indicates how much time an individual has to complete a task. A clock is typically running, signaling whether the individual is on pace to complete their task in the expected time.
- *Safety*: Safety is a leading indicator. If you can't get people on board with not getting hurt, it will be difficult to convince people to achieve high performance in other areas. Top performing companies have electronic boards at each location that shows how many days people have worked safely.

Daily Reports

These reports should be pushed out daily and made available in a manner that is appropriate for the people who need to see them. In some cases, email may not be available, so posting in a visible place or showing results on a display would be appropriate. Many companies have daily operations meetings to discuss issues and progress; these meetings are a good place to discuss progress.

- *Production*: This type of report shows good production against targets, and month to date versus target.
- *Sales*: This report shows how much was sold and at what price versus targets, and month to date versus target.
- *Cash*: This report shows how much was received (with top receipts broken out), how much was paid (with major disbursements broken out), and debt levels on one page.
- *Safety*: Number of recordable and lost time incidents should be reflected on daily automated reports to keep safety front and center.

Weekly Reports

These reports are in addition to the daily reports—which are focused on the building blocks to get to financial targets. The weekly reports are typically focused on working capital to ensure that working capital (accounts receivable and inventory) is not building. It also allows for progress against initiative or projects. These reports—coupled with the daily reports—would be included in an executive dashboard that gives a high-level perspective about whether the business is on track to achieve goals—and should be discussed in weekly senior management meetings.

- *Inventory*: This report highlights when a gap begins emerging between sales and production. There may be reasons to build inventory in advance of seasonal peaks. In most cases, the goal is not to have cash consumed by large amounts of inventory that may at some point be worthless.

- *Receivables*: Receivable collections can easily become problematic, as many people don't like to ask for payment. But, creating a culture of being paid in advance, having short terms, or being paid on time is not that difficult. If you are providing a valued product or service to your customers, being paid is not a challenge if you stay on top of it. Building receivables is basically financing your customer's business. Your margins probably don't have that built in.

- *Progress Against Schedule for Initiatives or Projects*: Every project has a critical path. There is always one timeline that either makes or breaks the overall project timeline. Tracking progress on each of the components that are to be completed that week, as well as the critical path, will determine whether the project comes in on time, on budget, and delivering the expected results. Usually, having a senior leader take part in the weekly meeting to challenge participants about deviations is the difference between schedule and budget slippage and delivering promised outcomes.

- *Sales Pipeline*: This report is a comprehensive view of the potential orders and their likelihood and timing. This allows for any gaps in orders to be identified and closed before a shortfall occurs. It also drives accountability for accurate forecasting and closing of orders.

Monthly Reports

These reports bring together the pieces being reviewed daily. They take a higher-level perspective—that is the basis for making course corrections in the business—as they show cross-functional views of results. Ideally, these reports would be reviewed by cross-functional teams to see what is going well and what needs to be done by whom to improve results.

- *Margin by Customer/Product*: Profitability is all about how much is produced and sold multiplied by the margin of those products. Many times, the amount produced and sold is measured carefully, but the related margin is not. It is important when looking at margins to ensure that there are not a number of allocations distorting the actual margins. Every month, the margin by customer and product should be reviewed by a cross-functional team. This allows the team to jointly determine whether sales prices need to be raised, costs reduced, or the product eliminated.

- *Financial Results (income statement, balance sheet, cash flow) Against Plan*: Financial results should be completed quickly—within a week of the end of the month—and circulated to managers in full. Financial results should never be a surprise. They should be a confirmation based on the activity throughout the month. Even though they are confirmations, they should be focal points of a monthly discussion of *what went well* and *what needs to happen* in the coming months to achieve growth targets.

- *Capital Expenditures Planned and Executed*: Capital expenditures are typically for either maintenance or strategic growth. Your capital budget should segregate between maintenance expenditures and those for strategic growth. Maintenance expenditures are necessary to keep your current business running. Strategic growth capital should have a return on investment through either increased production or reduced cost. Each month, the anticipated outcomes should be tracked to ensure the benefits are captured.

- *Return on Initiatives*: Most companies don't have an unlimited supply of funds to grow the business. So, when initiatives— typically an expense on the income statement—are identified as necessary to grow the business, their outcomes should be tracked to ensure the benefits expected are captured.

- *Banking Compliance, Including Covenants*: It is really easy to lose track of whether you are in compliance with your banking agreements, as seasonality and cyclicality may have a larger impact than you would expect. As part of monthly reporting, forecasted compliance certificates should be prepared to determine whether you are on track or corrective measures need to be taken.

References

Airbnb

Hoffman, R. 2017. "Handcrafted—Brian Chesky." *Masters of Scale.* https://mastersofscale.com/brian-chesky-handcrafted

Kessler, S. 2012. "How Snow White Helped Airbnb's Mobile Mission." *Fast Company.* https://www.fastcompany.com/3002813/how-snow-white-helped-airbnbs-mobile-mission

Amazon

Bezos, J. 2017. "2016 Letter to Shareholders." *Amazon.* https://www.amazon.com/p/feature/z6o9g6sysxur57t

Bloomberg, J. 2017. "Why Amazon Web Services is the Mother of All Candy Stores." *Forbes.* https://www.forbes.com/sites/jasonbloomberg/2017/12/03/why-amazon-web-services-is-the-mother-of-all-candy-stores/#8374ec55d189

Deutschman, A. 2004. "Inside the Mind of Jeff Bezos." *Fast Company.* https://www.fastcompany.com/50541/inside-mind-jeff-bezos-4

Gallo, H. 2017. "Cloud Market Keeps Growing at Over 40%; Amazon Still Increases Its Share." *Synergy Research Group.* https://www.srgresearch.com/articles/cloud-market-keeps-growing-over-40-amazon-still-increases-share

Landau, B. 2009. "Customer-Centricity with Amazon: An Interview with Bill Price, Former Global VP of Customer Service." *Customer Contact Week Digital.* https://www.customercontactweekdigital.com/strategy/interviews/customer-centricity-with-amazon-an-interview-with

Ramo, J. C. 1999. "Jeffrey Preston Bezos: 1999 Person of the Year." *Time.* http://content.time.com/time/subscriber/printout/0,8816,992927,00.html

Rose, C. December 1, 2013. "Amazon's Jeff Bezos Looks to the Future." *60 Minutes.* https://www.cbsnews.com/news/amazons-jeff-bezos-looks-to-the-future

Apple

Gallo, C. 2014. "The 7 Innovation Secrets of Steve Jobs." *Forbes.* https://www.forbes.com/sites/carminegallo/2014/05/02/the-7-innovation-secrets-of-steve-jobs/#4880e070751c

Ferris, T. October 14, 2017. "Lessons from Steve Jobs, Leonardo da Vinci, and Ben Franklin." *Tim Ferris Podcast.* https://tim.blog/2017/10/14/walter-isaacson

Wasik, J. 2016. "Apple Innovation Rules: Steve Jobs's Secrets." *Forbes.* https://www.forbes.com/sites/johnwasik/2016/05/20/apple-innovation-rules-steve-jobss-secrets/#324f06163a4b

Mark Fields

Eisenstein, P. 2017. "Did Ford Nix Its CEO Because He Was Too Much of a Visionary?" *NBC News.* https://www.nbcnews.com/business/autos/ford-s-fields-when-agent-change-trips-n763116

Hoffman, B. 2017. "Here's Why Ford's Mark Fields Had to Go." *Forbes.* https://www.forbes.com/sites/brycehoffman/2017/05/22/heres-why-fords-mark-fields-had-to-go/#723c01d43a92

Vlasic, B. 2017. "Ford, Trudging Into the Future, Ousts Mark Fields as C.E.O." *The New York Times.* https://www.nytimes.com/2017/05/22/business/ford-ceo-mark-fields-jim-hackett.html

Ford and Alan Mulally

Anonymous. 2007. "Ford Hit by Record $12.7bn Loss." *BBC.* http://news.bbc.co.uk/2/hi/business/6298463.stm

Baldoni, J. 2014. "Alan Mulally: Winning by Instilling Confidence." *Bloomberg.* https://www.forbes.com/sites/johnbaldoni/2014/04/23/alan-mulally-winning-by-instilling-confidence/#75e384c41f47

Birsel, A. 2017. "Love and be Loved, and Other Life Lessons from Alan Mulally," *Inc.* https://www.inc.com/ayse-birsel/3-lessons-i-learned-from-ford-ceo-alan-mulally-about-being-a-better-parent.html

Caldicott, S. M. 2014. "Why Ford's Alan Mulally is an Innovation CEO for the Record Books." *Forbes.* https://www.forbes.com/sites/

sarahcaldicott/2014/06/25/why-fords-alan-mulally-is-an-innovation-ceo-for-the-record-books/#71ea0dc27c04

Carey, D. 2011. "When finding the right CEO is Job #1." *Briefings Magazine.* https://www.kornferry.com/institute/11-when-finding-the-right-ceo-is-job-1

Carey and Keller, Fourth Quarter 2012, "How the Ford board recruited Alan Mulally," *Directors & Boards*, pp. 31–36.

Edersheim, E. H. 2016. "Alan Mulally, Ford, and the 6Cs." *Brookings.* https://www.brookings.edu/blog/education-plus-development/2016/06/28/alan-mulally-ford-and-the-6cs

Ford Motor Company Historical Data. *ADVFN.* https://www.advfn.com/stock-market/NYSE/F/historical

Glenn, M. 2015. "Marshall Goldsmith: Lessons from a Top Executive Coach." *IBM.com.* https://www.ibm.com/blogs/insights-on-business/ibmix/marshall-goldsmith

Goldsmith, M. 2015. "What Successful People Know that You Need to Learn!" *Marshall Goldsmith Personal Blog.* http://www.marshallgoldsmithfeedforward.com/marshallgoldsmithblog/?p=980

Gray, T. 2013. "How A Painting From 1925 Inspired Ford's Customer-Focused Future." *Fast Company.* https://www.fastcompany.com/3012809/how-a-painting-from-1925-inspired-fords-customer-focused-future

Hoffman, B. 2012. "Saving An Iconic Brand: Five Ways Alan Mulally Changed Ford's Culture." *Fast Company.* https://www.fastcompany.com/1680075/saving-an-iconic-brand-five-ways-alan-mulally-changed-ford-s-culture

Kirkland, R. 2013. "Leading in the 21st century: An Interview with Ford's Alan Mulally." *McKinsey&Company.* https://www.mckinsey.com/business-functions/strategy-and-corporate-finance/our-insights/leading-in-the-21st-century-an-interview-with-fords-alan-mulally

Kurtzman, J., and M. Distefano. 2014. "Alan Mulally: The Man Who Saved Ford." *Briefings Magazine.* https://www.kornferry.com/institute/alan-mulally-man-who-saved-ford

Looi, S. 2010. "Ford: The Remake of an American Icon." *Forbes.* https://www.forbes.com/sites/greatspeculations/2010/11/08/ford-the-remake-of-an-american-icon/#2c562c5f108c

Mahanta, V., and S. Vijakakumar. 2014. "Ford CEO Alan Mulally on Scripting One of the Most Incredible Turnarounds in Corporate History." *The Economic Times.* https://economictimes.indiatimes.com/ magazines/corporate-dossier/ford-ceo-alan-mulally-on-scripting- one-of-the-most-incredible-turnarounds-in-corporate-history/ printarticle/37253383.cms

Nocera, J. 2017. "Ford Sees New CEO as Second Coming of Alan Mulally." *Bloomberg.* https://www.bloomberg.com/view/articles/2017-05-23/ ford-sees-new-ceo-as-second-coming-of-alan-mulally

Stallard, M.L. 2014. "7 Practices of Alan Mulally that Helped For Pass Competitors." *FoxBusiness.* https://www.foxbusiness.com/fox-business/ 7-practices-of-alan-mulally-that-helped-ford-pass-competitors

Vlasic, B. 2009. "Choosing Its Own Path, Ford Stayed Independent." *The New York Times.* http://www.nytimes.com/2009/04/09/business/ 09ford.html?pagewanted=all&_r=0

Ben Franklin

Anonymous. 2002. "Man of Letters." *PBS.* http://www.pbs.org/benfranklin/ 13_world_letters.html

Barthel, M. 2017. "Despite Subscription Surges for Largest U.S. Newspapers, Circulation and Revenue Fall for Industry Overall." *Pew Research Center.* http://www.pewresearch.org/fact-tank/2017/06/01/circulation- and-revenue-fall-for-newspaper-industry

Ferris, T. October 14, 2017. "Lessons from Steve Jobs, Leonardo da Vinci, and Ben Franklin." *Tim Ferris Podcast.* https://tim.blog/2017/10/14/ walter-isaacson

U.S. Post office Benjamin Franklin, Postmaster General. https://about .usps.com/who-we-are/postal-history/pmg-franklin.pdf

General Electric

Egan, M. 2017. "How Decades of Bad Decisions Broke G.E." *CNN Money.* http://money.cnn.com/2017/11/20/investing/general-electric- immelt-what-went-wrong/index.html

V.V.V. November 30, 2017. "Why General Electric Is Struggling." *The Economist.* https://www.economist.com/blogs/economist-explains/2017/11/economist-explains-21

Abraham Lincoln

Goodwin, D. K. 2005. *Team of Rivals: The Political Genius of Abraham Lincoln.* New York: Simon & Schuster.

Shenk, J. 2005. "Lincoln's Great Depression." *The Atlantic.* https://www.theatlantic.com/magazine/archive/2005/10/lincolns-great-depression/304247

McDonald's Cantalupo and Bell

Howard, T. 2004. "McDonald's Chief Cantalupo Dies; Bell Is Successor." *USA Today.* http://usatoday30.usatoday.com/money/industries/food/2004-04-19-cantalupo_x.htm

Saxon, W. 2004. "James R. Cantalupo, Chief of McDonald's, Is Dead at 60." *The New York Times.* http://www.nytimes.com/2004/04/20/business/james-r-cantalupo-chief-of-mcdonald-s-is-dead-at-60.html

Sellers, P. 2011. "How McDonald's Got CEO Succession Right." *Fortune.* http://fortune.com/2011/08/23/how-mcdonalds-got-ceo-succession-right

Warner, M. 2005. "Charles Bell, 44, Former Chief Executive of McDonald's, Dies." *The New York Times.* http://www.nytimes.com/2005/01/17/obituaries/charles-bell-44-former-chief-executive-of-mcdonalds-dies.html

Oscar Munoz

Peck, E. 2015. "United CEO's Heart Attack Underscores Health Hazards of Stress." *HuffPost.* http://www.huffingtonpost.com/entry/oscar-munoz-united-heart-attack-stress_us_562e6afee4b06317990ec183

Zhang, B. 2017. "United Airlines CEO Nearly Died a Month Into the Job—Here's the One Piece of Health Advice that Saved His Life." *Business Insider.* http://www.businessinsider.com/united-airlines-ceo-health-advice-saved-his-life-2017-3

Jacques Nasser

Anonymous. November 1, 2001. "The Shake-up at Ford: Jacques Knifed." *The Economist.* https://www.economist.com/node/842705

Taylor III, A. 2001. "What's Behind Ford's Fall? Late Products, Lousy Sales, Low Morale—and It Doesn't Help that the Top Guys Have Different Agendas." *Fortune.* http://archive.fortune.com/magazines/fortune/fortune_archive/2001/10/29/312418/index.htm

Netflix

Dunn, J. 2017. "Here's How Huge Netflix Has Gotten in the Past Decade." *Business Insider.* http://www.businessinsider.com/netflix-subscribers-chart-2017-1

Hoffman, R. 2017. "Culture Shock—Reed Hastings." *Masters of Scale Podcast.* https://mastersofscale.com/reed-hastings-culture-shock

TOMS

Ferris, T. June 28, 2017. "How to Make a Difference and Find Your Purpose—Blake Mycoskie." *Tim Ferris Podcast.* https://tim.blog/2017/06/28/blake-mycoskie

Hoffman, R. 2017. "Imperfect is Perfect—Mark Zuckerberg." *Masters of Scale.* https://mastersofscale.com/mark-zuckerberg-imperfect-is-perfect

Isaza, M., and L. Italie. May 13, 2016. "60 million pairs of shoes and 10 years later: Toms Shoes founder reflects." *The Seattle Times.* https://www.seattletimes.com/life/fashion/60-million-pairs-of-shoes-and-10-years-later-toms-shoes-founder-reflects

Other References

Griffin, M. "10 Health Problems Related to Stress That You Can Fix." *WebMD.* http://www.webmd.com/balance/stress-management/features/10-fixable-stress-related-health-problems#1

Grunbaum, R. December 4, 2010. "Longview Fibre Now a 'Textbook Example' of Revival." *The Seattle Times.* http://old.seattletimes.com/html/sundaybuzz/2013582135_sundaybuzz05.html

Mochari, I. March 23, 2016. "Why Half of the S&P 500 Companies Will Be Replaced in the Next Decade." *Inc.* https://www.inc.com/ilan-mochari/innosight-sp-500-new-companies.html

Perry, M. August 18, 2014. "Fortune 500 firms in 1955 vs. 2014; 88% are gone, and we're all better off because of that dynamic 'creative destruction'." *AEI.* http://www.aei.org/publication/fortune-500-firms-in-1955-vs-2014-89-are-gone-and-were-all-better-off-because-of-that-dynamic-creative-destruction

About the Author

Heidi Pozzo is a leadership and high-performance expert. She helps C-suite leaders and boards dramatically increase their organizations' value. With 20 years of strategic, financial, and operational experience in her role as trusted advisor and expert, Heidi has a unique background that allows her to quickly grasp both the strategic and the operational. She helped engineer the turnaround of an $800-million organization, which Deutsche Bank analyst Mark Wilde called "the best turnaround case study we have seen in . . . 25 years." *Portland Business Journal* recognized Heidi's work, naming her "CFO of the Year—Large Company."

Heidi serves as Association for Corporate Growth, Portland Chapter, treasurer and is on the Board Nominating Committee for the Girl Scouts of Oregon and Southwest Washington. She recently served on the Board of Directors for Big Brothers Big Sisters, Columbia Northwest, various committees at Multnomah Athletic Club, and the Graphic Arts Council Board of the Portland Art Museum.

Heidi has worked in more than 20 industries, including manufacturing, construction, procurement, engineering, forest products, and business services. She holds a bachelor of science degree in business administration from California State Polytechnic University, Pomona, and a master's degree in business administration from Rice University.

You can reach Heidi at:
Website: heidipozzo.com;
email: heidi@heidipozzo.com

Index

OTHER TITLES IN THE HUMAN RESOURCE MANAGEMENT AND ORGANIZATIONAL BEHAVIOR COLLECTION

- *Conflict and Leadership: How to Harness the Power of Conflict to Create Better Leaders and Build Thriving Teams* by Christian Muntean
- *Creating the Accountability Culture: The Science of Life Changing Leadership* by Yvonnne Thompson
- *Managing Organizational Change: The Measurable Benefits of Applied iOCM* by Linda C. Mattingly
- *Precision Recruitment Skills: How to Find the Right Person For the Right Job, the First Time* by Rod Matthews
- *Practical Performance Improvement: How to Be an Exceptional People Manager* by Rod Matthews
- *Creating Leadership: How to Change Hippos Into Gazelles* by Philip Goodwin and Tony Page
- *Uncovering the Psychology of Good Bosses vs Bad Bosses and What it Means for Leaders: How to Avoid the High Cost of Bad Leadership* by Debra Dupree
- *Competency Based Education: How to Prepare College Graduates for the World of Work* by Nina Morel and Bruce Griffiths
- *Phenomenology and Its Application in Business* by Roger Sages and Abhishek Goel
- *Organizational Design in Business: A New Alternative for a Complex World* by Carrie Foster
- *The 360 Degree CEO: Generating Profits While Leading and Living with Passion and Principles* by Lorraine A. Moore

Announcing the Business Expert Press Digital Library

Concise e-books business students need for classroom and research

This book can also be purchased in an e-book collection by your library as

- *a one-time purchase,*
- *that is owned forever,*
- *allows for simultaneous readers,*
- *has no restrictions on printing, and*
- *can be downloaded as PDFs from within the library community.*

Our digital library collections are a great solution to beat the rising cost of textbooks. E-books can be loaded into their course management systems or onto students' e-book readers. The **Business Expert Press** digital libraries are very affordable, with no obligation to buy in future years. For more information, please visit **www.businessexpertpress.com/librarians**. To set up a trial in the United States, please email **sales@businessexpertpress.com**.

CPSIA information can be obtained
at www.ICGtesting.com
Printed in the USA
FFHW01n1102230718
47496395-50815FF